BEYOND STORMY WEATHER

Keys to Understanding, Navigating and Embracing Your Emotions

CHRISTINE JUDD

First published by Ultimate World Publishing 2020
Copyright © 2020 Christine Judd

ISBN

Paperback: 978-1-922372-96-3
Ebook: 978-1-922372-97-0

Cover design: Ultimate World Publishing
Layout and typesetting: Ultimate World Publishing
Editor: Marinda Wilkinson
Cover illustration: Andrii Stepaniuk-Shutterstock.com
Illustrations: Phil Judd www.comic-express.com

Ultimate World Publishing
Diamond Creek,
Victoria Australia 3089
www.writeabook.com.au

Dedication

To my mother and father, John and Beryl, for instilling in me a love for reading and learning.

To my brother Phillip, for his ongoing support and care, and deep understanding of the creative process.

Contents

Dedication   iii

Foreword   vii

Introduction   ix

Chapter 1: Stormy Weather   3

Chapter 2: The Relentless Flow   19

Chapter 3: Mind the Gap   37

Chapter 4: Luck of the Draw   59

Chapter 5: Safe Harbour in the Storm   77

Chapter 6: Cultivating Grounding   93

Chapter 7: Habits, Habits, Habits   109

Chapter 8: Relationship to Self   129

Chapter 9: Relationship with Others   147

Chapter 10: Harvesting the Riches   167

Afterword   185

References   187

Author Bio   189

Foreword

Stop being emotional!

You are too emotional!

She is just being emotional!

As a young woman these were phrases that I heard often. Back then, emotions were negative, something I ultimately worked hard at hiding from others and myself. If I felt happy, I would feel guilty. If I felt sad, I would feel shame.

Over the years, I have rediscovered my emotional self, and this has been key to finding me and my true path. It wasn't easy to face my emotional self again and it took years to finally break through and embrace the emotional me.

Now as I look back at the younger me, I wish I had access to this book then. I would have found me earlier and been further along my true path. Instead of feeling guilt and shame, I would have been able to truly be in the moment, of happiness and sadness, all emotions that I now embrace completely.

Christine takes us on a powerful journey of self-discovery as we learn to value our emotions. Step by step your appreciation of emotions will grow as you gain valuable insights. As I worked through this book, I revisited events in my life from long ago, that I hadn't realised were still having a huge impact on my life now. As I took that journey back, my appreciation and understanding of the events and more importantly my emotional responses at the time became clearer. With that newfound clarity, I heard the messages behind my emotions and saw the events through new eyes.

The beauty of this book is that you are encouraged to take the opportunity to stop and reflect. In a world where we are all too busy for this and that, never be too busy for you. Follow Christine's guidance and stop, take the opportunity to fully experience each reflection point and practice point. You owe it to yourself, to understand your emotions, embrace your emotions and learn from your emotions.

In this book Christine talks about mindfulness, and as I write this foreword I revisit the experience I had from reading and I feel myself grow taller in my seat, my shoulders pull back and a smile comes across my face. I hear in my mind, 'Yes! This is Me!' and I am bursting with emotions—happiness, determination, joy, hope, love, motivation, optimism, pride … That is the magic of connecting with your emotions.

As a Holistic Life and Communication Coach, I work with clients who struggle with their emotions and the limiting beliefs linked to their emotional past, and I have witnessed firsthand the extraordinary changes that embracing your emotional self can have.

I am excited to add *Beyond Stormy Weather* to my recommended reading for my clients as I have experienced and know the value of the learnings provided by Christine.

Kaylene Ledgar,
Author and Holistic Life and Communication Coach

Introduction

Emotions are complex and uniquely individual. In over twenty years of working with thousands of people from a myriad of backgrounds, whether one-off meetings or longer term therapeutic work, I remain constantly amazed at the way in which a person, their life and the concerns that they present with, are so individual. No two are alike. There are many shared issues and circumstances, however, the way in which we respond, thrive and survive remains incomparable. It is what keeps the work I do alive and interesting. It makes for a colourful and special journey to share with others when they are speaking about their own story and life experiences. It is also a constant reminder to myself to never assume, presume or project my own particular story with my emotions onto others, despite the seeming similarities.

Writing a book on emotions and tips for being with our emotions that is for general consumption, is therefore an ambitious and slightly perilous project to embark on. Drawing on a weather analogy when I have no background in science specifically or meteorology is equally questionable. However, the spirit of this book and how it can be of assistance goes like this ...

First and foremost, it is ultimately up to you to judge or discern what is helpful, what are the areas around your emotions that you identify as benefiting from focus and questioning, and how you might use the ideas within this book. This is a book of ideas gathered from training and experience. It is drawn from professional and personal experience, but nevertheless it is an offering. There are no directives, no hard and fast rules. If anything, it seeks to stimulate seeking out the parts of your puzzle that fit together, if there is a puzzle around your emotional life to be solved.

WHO IS THIS BOOK FOR?

The aim of this book is to assist people who experience intense emotions and are troubled by them, who frequently feel the extreme ends of the emotional spectrum—emotionally stormy weather.

The experience that usually accompanies this storminess includes feeling overwhelmed or flooded by emotions, swamped, struggling to manage your emotional state, mired down in feelings and dominated by emotion. A term I use with clients, to check in around their own experience of this, is if they feel they get 'hijacked' by their feelings. By this I mean the emotion takes over to the absence of all else, and it can seem like there is absolutely no choice in the matter—they feel in the grip of the emotion. This usually exacerbates the feelings and adds to them (which will be focused on later as an intensifying process).

When you experience intense emotional storms frequently, aspects of your development and sense of self can be railroaded. It feels extremely uncomfortable and stressful—it is the system under stress. The strong emotions eclipse all else, which makes getting on with life and functioning difficult.

Emotional storms can also:
- take away your ability to focus
- be extremely draining and exhausting
- make you feel out of control, hence 'hijacked'
- affect your relationships in a detrimental way
- change your perception of the world, distorting your sense of reality

- affect your relationship with yourself and your self-confidence and trust.

If you do not feel troubled by your feelings and emotions in this way, if the need for a book on this makes you scratch your head in confusion, then you are probably not experiencing the emotional storms that this book aims to assist with. It is akin to being healthy and not consciously noticing the body due to an absence of pain or strain. Or like being in moderate weather where, again, there is no need to consciously focus on the elements as they do not impact you greatly.

The other reason a person may not need this book is if they already have the resources and skills covered in the book to handle their emotions confidently. If you have already acquired these through life experience or from your own hard work to learn and develop them, this book may further affirm these skills for you.

SUGGESTIONS ON HOW TO USE THIS BOOK

Doing it freestyle

My favourite way of learning and picking up on information that serves me, is what I call 'doing it freestyle'. I am not a great fan of structure (although it tends to benefit me) and I like a feeling of freedom and space when I do things. So the first suggestion in how to use this book is: read the book (brilliant, I know) and if anything resonates—provides an insight into yourself, stirs some interest or creates an increased perspective of truth—then ... make a note of it. Jot it down. Collect it like a bowerbird might collect objects that it finds and take it back to your nest.

Some practical suggestions for ordering the valuable moments of the book include:

- creating a journal where you gather anything that speaks to you
- writing down page numbers of sections you'd like to refer back to

- recording the names of theories or models that may be valuable.

Create a personal resource book

If the focus of this book—stormy emotional experience—is an issue, collecting practices, insights, information, further resources and ideas more formally and with clear intention, can be an extremely valuable enterprise.

Create a personal emotional resources file book that you continue building on as you explore and find helpful ideas and practices. Be creative about it but also efficient: it might be a specially chosen journal; it might be a shoebox full of scraps of paper ... but collect.

HOW THIS BOOK IS STRUCTURED

Throughout each chapter there are a couple of recurring sections which offer ways to make the material presented your own. The idea of this book is to ultimately benefit you in your emotional world.

The recurring sections are:

Key Concept: This represents a basic and important concept or idea.

Reflection Points: The questions posed in these points are designed to help deepen understanding of the chapter topic and connect it to your own life.

Practice Points: These are where actual strategies are described that can be put into practice during your day. They are simple, varying from something that can be implemented on the go to more formal practices where carving out a certain amount of time is recommended.

In Summary: At the end of each chapter a summary of the area of focus is succinctly repeated, to remind you of the key point and the reason it can be of benefit.

Takeaway Practices: At the end of each chapter you'll find suggestions on how you can begin to use or explore some of the ideas and strategies described, within your daily life.

Please note that if you have a diagnosed mental health condition or have persistent distress, assessment and treatment from a mental health professional is advised. This can be accessed through your GP. No book can replace individualised professional mental health treatment. The information provided in this book is general in nature and may complement support strategies offered in such treatment. Equally, if working through the material in this book alone is not right for you, please seek the support of a counsellor or therapist.

A FINAL WORD ...

A final point on using this book is that it covers a broad range of topics relevant to understanding, navigating and embracing emotions we all experience. Each chapter covers off an area that I have found to be important in handling the emotional side of being human, as reiterated by people I have worked with as well as my personal experience. They are all tried and true ideas, concepts, practices and approaches; but how they are covered in this book is undoubtedly brief.

Thus, the final word is, that if any of the key areas of a chapter feel particularly helpful and significant to you, research them further. There will be other books and articles where the topic is covered more extensively than is possible here. Use any discoveries sparked through this book to guide your next steps—to spur on your journey of self-discovery, self-understanding and of coming into a new relationship with your feelings.

'I am not afraid of storms, for I am learning how to sail my ship.'

Louisa May Alcott

CHAPTER 1

Stormy Weather

I have mixed feelings about storms.

On one hand, the idea of a severe weather warning or gloomy forecast, of dramatic winds and rain, lightning and thunder, sudden shifts in the natural light and temperature, the sensation and sound of a storm whipping across the land, injects a sense of excitement and aliveness in me. As a child, I remember the anticipation of watching developing storms with my mother and brother out on our back veranda, safe and settled in comfortably together, ready to witness the natural spectacle of the unpredictable, wild sky show before us.

In those moments, nature was wonderful; I was safe with my family, and we were part of something clearly way beyond us in size, force and scale.

This excitement was felt through my whole physical body. The senses came alive with the smell of rain imbued the dust, the feel of the wetness of the rain and force of the wind, the sudden visible crack of lightning and deep, visceral rumble of thunder, a dramatic clattering of rain pouring down on the tin roof. It all made me feel part of something unequivocally bigger than myself, with a life force and energy of its own. It was exhilarating on so many levels. Living in a small town in a vast, dry country also meant that any prospect of rain held an added value. From the simple view of a young country girl, rain was a significant and positive thing where I came from, and it made the adults and community as a whole incredibly happy.

So, for me personally, storms evoke a certain feeling and attitude. They have also become associated with memories of family, the wonder of childhood, and an awe and love of nature—all positive sentiments.

But on the other hand, I can see the broader reality that comes with facing the might of storms. If I experienced a storm where water flooded my home and community, destroying my security, housing and treasured possessions, threatening my life and the lives of my loved ones, I would feel very differently. If I lived in the cyclone areas of Northern Australia or the tornado belt in middle America, or if I was Gilligan, Skipper, Ginger or the Howells in the 60s American sitcom, caught on the SS Minnow in a sudden tropical storm that left me shipwrecked for years, an impending storm would feel far more ominous. And for this reason, I do feel a little guilty about the excitement that a prospective storm brings.

The dangers of the storm, of lightning never seemed too real as a kid, but I heard the message: caught out on the golf course with my father and brother with shiny metal sticks was a big no-no, standing under a tree during a storm had mixed reviews (shelter from the lightning was needed but at the same time lightning frequently felled trees in a cracking display).

Thus, we could put it this way: I have thankfully never been at the mercy of a major storm. However, when we talk about emotional storms, upon which this book is focused, it is another story altogether ...

So, what on earth does stormy weather have to do with emotions?

EMOTIONAL STORMY WEATHER

Emotions have been likened to weather for many centuries and there are definite parallels. From cultural and spiritual practices, to the arts and literature, they are often connected in a symbolic or metaphoric way.

Different forms of weather often provide certain types of mood and moodiness and have become connected with certain emotions and emotional states. Think of the beginning of *The Rocky Horror Picture Show* with the car broken down in the storm. It conveyed a clear sense of impending doom and danger for the stranded couple, albeit, tongue-in-cheek. Equally, the way weather is unpredictable, coming and going, shifting and changing, yet simultaneously alive and energetic, is similar to the qualities of our emotions and emotional lives.

Emotions, as with weather, also occur along a continuum of intensity. We tend to notice feelings at the extremes as we do with weather at the extremes. With mild weather, we are not so impacted and will barely even consciously register conditions if we don't need to do anything in response to them. Similarly, people may long for the days of good health if they are injured, sick or develop a condition—but while healthy, there can be an absence of feeling of the physical body, a lightness and simplicity in the experience of it. It works. It functions. It does as you want it to, and you are symptom-free.

In the same way, it is the impacts (or potential impacts) of weather that draw our conscious attention to it, compelling us to respond to the conditions. And so it is with emotions—intense, wild, extreme emotions compel us to face them and deal with them.

But what exactly do I mean when I talk about emotions?

KEY CONCEPTS: Emotions Defined

Emotions can be defined as an event we experience within our private self. In psychology, it is recognised as a complex phenomenon, an internal state of feeling that produces physical and psychological changes that affect our behaviour and thoughts. Words to indicate emotions are often used interchangeably and include *emotion*, *feeling*, *mood*, and in psychology, *affect*, to describe them.

Here's a quick breakdown of terms:

Emotion: a complex psychological state that includes physiological and psychological changes in response to an identifiable stimulus, as an intense but short-lived event. It can include thoughts, feelings and behaviour urges.

Feeling: a subjective experience of emotion, focused in the body.

Mood: a sustained and pervasive emotional state that is not linked to an identifiable trigger or may be the accumulation of multiple contributing factors. A mood can last from several hours to days or weeks. It provides an underlying emotional tone, that can colour perceptions of the world.

Affect: used in psychology to name observable emotion and feeling, as demonstrated through demeanour, body, face, tone of voice and verbal expression.

THE LIVED EXPERIENCE OF EMOTION

In this book I refer to the experience of feeling and emotion without being too technical about scientific definitions, or the ongoing scientific endeavour to define and understand them. I am interested in and address the 'lived experience' of your feelings with the ideas, information and practices presented. That is because we are all familiar with our own emotional experiences—our 'emotional selves' as I refer to throughout this book. I borrow the phrase 'lived experience' from other areas in the field of mental health that focus on the day-to-day reality of an aspect of our mental health, rather than the more formal, diagnostic, theoretical and academic aspects of them.

The strength of focusing on the lived experience is that you as the person, the 'feeler', are the expert in your own life. And your own perception of your emotion matters: it is the reality and it holds authority because it is what you experience. Certainly, throughout this book I will also refer to some of those other aspects where it seems relevant and helpful, most often drawn from psychology and biological science, but the main focus of this book is on the everyday lived experience of emotions for the reader.

THE SPECTRUM OF EMOTIONS

There are a variety of emotions and feelings, and we utilise language to name them, indicating and labelling what we are experiencing.

Below is a list of some of the common emotions and feelings that may be experienced. Read through them and see how you relate to them. There may be some that you recognise readily and there may be others that feel more foreign to your lived experience.

List of Emotions

Afraid	Aggrieved	Anxious
Angry	Annoyed	Ashamed
Bereft	Bored	Bitter
Confused	Content	Depressed
Determined	Disgusted	Embarrassed
Envious	Frustrated	Furious
Happy	Hopeful	Hurt
Inadequate	Insecure	Inspired
Intimidated	Jealous	Joyful
Lonely	Loved/loving	Miserable
Motivated	Nervous	Numb
Overwhelmed	Optimistic	Peaceful
Pessimistic	Proud	Relieved
Resentful	Sad	Satisfied
Scared	Self-conscious	Shocked

List of Emotions (continued)

Suspicious	Tense	Terrified
Trapped	Uncomfortable	Worried
Worthless		

This list is by no means exhaustive. You may think of some that aren't listed, (or where the name differs to what you personally use) but it is a helpful starting point to begin thinking about your emotional self and the broad variety of emotional experiences possible.

REFLECTION POINT

Look through the emotion list and identify emotions you feel familiar with, emotions that you may never experience, emotions you are comfortable with and the ones that make you uncomfortable. Make a mental note of how you respond to the range of emotions on this list. Add in any missing for you.

SUBJECTIVE OR OBJECTIVE? NAMING AND CATEGORISING EMOTIONS

The inner experience of emotions and feelings are subjective in terms of how they are felt and the name you might find fits best. They are part of our own inner, private world that only we have access to.

However, there are common, seemingly shared human experiences of types of feeling that language and theory has attempted to capture. Several theories have proposed 'basic emotions' common to all people.

Pioneering emotional theorist and professor in psychology, Robert Plutichik, identified eight main emotions that he proposed could be paired in opposites:

- joy versus sorrow
- anger versus fear
- acceptance versus disgust
- surprise versus expectancy.

8

He likened distinguishing different emotions to identifying different colours and created a visual representation, his famous 'emotion wheel', to present his ideas. Other theories have challenged Plutichik's ideas, presenting different numbers of 'core' emotions and 'secondary' emotions. The quest to quantify the number of emotions and categories, to understand emotions generally, remains an area of increased and ongoing scientific activity. It is also recognised that in different cultures, concepts and words for feelings vary.

In some languages certain feelings are not identified, and other feelings might have multiple words that describe different nuances of it. For example, neuroscientist and psychologist Lisa Feldman Barrett identified forty-six words in Gaelic that are variations of the feeling of sadness.

With science proposing varied theories, the range and nature of feelings remains unresolved. Add to this, the cultural and linguistic variation in identifying emotions, and the subjective side of this topic is evident.

Ultimately, it is for you to identify and give a word to what you feel, as a helpful way of acknowledging and understanding it. Language and labelling can assist us in making sense intellectually of our experience and assist in communicating our feelings to others. Ultimately, we are experts of our own reality and must call it in a way that makes sense to us.

Why do I care so much about emotions?

I have had a long history with emotional storms that has shaped the course of my life significantly, to the point where I became a therapist and social worker in order to delve into the whole world of emotions more deeply—learning and applying my new skills on a personal level first and foremost. This could be called self-help with a hefty student loan and a career afterwards.

By gaining a solid foundation of psychology research, and training in techniques and different modalities of working therapeutically with emotions, I aimed to address the storminess within: to understand better, to navigate better and ultimately embrace the benefits of the emotions that I struggled with so fiercely at times. I was driven to seek answers from the inside out, to assist myself, to evolve and develop my own capacity to manage my emotional self. Along this path, I ultimately came to understand how misunderstood our emotions, our emotional selves and lives are, way beyond my own skin. And I came to understand how much it matters.

I tapped into a genuine interest and appreciation of others and their stories (which were frequently vastly different to mine) and a passion grew to support those who were struggling in their own way to handle emotions. I learned there are many types of storms and a multitude of rich, significant stories that accompany them.

In working with hundreds of people from a variety of backgrounds and circumstances, the one thing that is clear to me is that the experience of emotions and the emotional self is a uniquely individual one. No two people are exactly alike; there certainly may be similarities and patterns that are common to people, where two people may resonate with each other's stories and share similar experiences, but nevertheless, the individual is unique.

I was able to appreciate the contributing factors in my own emotional storms: significant experiences of grief and loss early in life, including both parents, a lack of clear guidance around managing my emotions, biological vulnerabilities that have led to my having formal diagnoses of both depression and anxiety, as well as not accessing professional support for a number of years as a young person (times were different then with less mental health services available, and stigma and mystery surrounding such services).

So, an important point for you to remember is, that you are unique, and it is only your truth around emotions that matters as you read. There is no right or wrong in looking at our emotions. Rather, it is essential to strive to identify your own particular truth. As you read this book you will be asked to do reflective exercises at certain points, to begin to make these ideas and practices your own, and to assist with understanding your truth more readily.

Give yourself the freedom to be as open and honest as you are comfortable with, so you can build greater self-understanding around your own emotional world.

KEY CONCEPT: Emotions as Positive or Negative

Emotions routinely get classified as negative and positive, and this simply reflects how desirable they may be to humans. However, the fact is that to feel and have emotions, opens us to the whole range of feelings—we cannot cherrypick our emotions and say, 'I will have these ones and not those ones, thanks very much'. Certainly, if that were possible, wouldn't it have worked for us all already?

To feel is to be alive and impacted by life; all emotions have a role to play and a potential to be felt. All emotions have value, no matter how difficult the experience of them may feel. In the same way we cannot have light without dark, warm without cool, silence without sound; similarly, we cannot know joy without sadness, peace without agitation, love without grief. To numb down one feeling tends to numb down all feeling in a blanket way … and to feel allows all feeling to come.

So, as you read, see if you can open your mind to all emotions being of worth, value and beneficial experiences.

THE ROLE OF THE FIGHT-OR-FLIGHT RESPONSE WITH EMOTIONS

Let's explore another important element of what underlies the desirability or the undesirability of an emotion and feeling. This has a great amount to do with a biological system in all mammals including humans. And it also has a great deal to do with the set-up and experience of emotional storms.

KEY CONCEPT: The Fight-or-Flight Response

The fight-or-flight response (sometimes called the stress response) is important in understanding what can activate intense emotions within and play an ongoing role in perpetuating emotional storms.

As part of early human evolution, our survival as a species depended upon the development of an in-built physiological and psychological mechanism that activates instantaneously when we perceive danger, a threat or a risk to our survival within our environment. This is called our fight-or-flight response. We need to be able to rapidly respond to dangers without our usual mode of operating placing us at peril by the amount of time it takes to process information and respond. Survival was, and is, not a leisurely, contemplative thing.

The fight-or-flight response is designed to allow us to switch into several options:

- to fight off the threat
- to flee from the danger
- to go into a freeze response.

This freeze response is a later addition to the fight-or-flight response, identified as a third option. It occurs where the danger of fleeing or fighting is perceived as too perilous or impossible, and that freezing in situ, staying still, is necessary to minimise harm. In this freeze state the same mechanisms for a shift into fight or flight remain, as an ongoing potential action to take if the opportunity comes.

So, this biological response overrides all other systems and daily functions within, to maximise a rapid response to perceived threats. The brain regulates the body and where energy needs to be invested at each given time, according to information received through our senses.

During this response, a flood of hormones are released that have a number of effects on the body. Breathing increases so that we have maximum oxygen for access to energy, the heart rate and blood pressure rapidly increases to raise blood flow and carrying of oxygen to where it is needed, blood is pumped to our limbs for a rapid physical response via our muscles and blood is moved away from other areas of the body such as digestion. The body also looks to remove any other impediments—the kind of familiar response that can happen to some before exams, a job interview, giving a speech, or facing someone we fear or feel unsafe around. Perspiration can occur to cool us off and maintain temperature while potentially being highly active, and the normal thinking processes are suspended.

This response commonly raises feelings of terror, fear, shock, pain, anger and aggression, as part of the triggering of this response, and if not during, as after-effects of a stressful event.

Which now leads us to the connection between the fight-or-flight response and why a person can struggle with their emotions and feel them problematic to manage in their lives.

WHY DO PEOPLE EXPERIENCE EMOTIONAL STORMS?

In my years as a therapist, it is precisely emotions which lead people to seek out professional help. It is emotional struggle, pain and difficulty that matters and instigates a reaching out for help around normally privately held matters.

The main reasons I have come to recognise as leading people to experience emotional storms are one, or more often, a combination of the following factors:

- current events in life
- past events in life
- biological vulnerabilities
- a lack of knowledge, skills, experience
- a lack of confidence.

Let's have a look at each of these more closely.

Current events in life

We all know that in life, adversities happen. Things that we do not want, happen. Often things that we don't expect to happen, occur, and that can cause significant, painful emotions. These type of things can include conflict with loved ones and others who are significant to us, the death of someone or the loss of something important in our life, changes forced upon us, and times in our lives where there is a high demand upon us.

There is a famous study from 1967 that researched the most stressful events that people can go through, rating their significance to experiencing stress. The researchers, Holmes and Rahe, came up with a scale that rated the 'units of change' of each type of life event. A scale was designed to screen people for significant life events affecting stress levels and health. It was called the Social Readjustment Rating Scale, and clearly acknowledged how life changes matter and have a meaningful bearing on health.

The following were the top ten highest rating events, in order:
- death of a spouse
- divorce
- marital separation
- imprisonment
- death of a close family member
- personal injury or illness
- marriage
- dismissal from work
- marital reconciliation
- retirement.

While this is an older study and based on research in a Western-based cultural setting, it indicates some of the common occurrences that can have an impact on health including our emotional wellbeing.

The fact is, that events of life naturally impact our emotional state and sense of wellbeing. These events involve change and place demands upon us emotionally and psychologically. In our modern lives, it is precisely these types of changes or steps into the unfamiliar, that can trigger a fight-or-flight response in us.

We can feel at risk in new, difficult, and challenging circumstances. Other events to consider include experiences of violence in all forms and other traumatic events.

To not be affected by significant changes in life and have emotions arise in response to these events would be unusual.

Past events in life

The impacts of past life events that were emotionally activating and significant at the time can remain present and get triggered in current life in many ways. These include the same type of events as covered in current life events but are often experiences where the emotions were not able to be processed at the time.

Difficulty processing emotions can occur for a variety of reasons including: the age at the time of occurrence and the maturity of the person emotionally, having the emotional skills to deal with the challenging event and response to it, and the type of reactions and support of the people around you (or lack of).

Past life events can have a continuing effect on a person after the event and it is not uncommon to be affected for decades. Past events can represent particularly complex activations of the fight-or-flight response that may not get resolved and therefore prime us for ongoing emotional sensitivity and subsequent storminess. Traumatic events are included in this.

Biological factors

There are several angles to consider around being emotionally vulnerable that may stem from individual biological and genetic make-up.

'Vulnerability' means a greater susceptibility to or an increased potential for something to occur. In this regard everyone is different, and differences need to be acknowledged. For some people there is a biological predisposition to feeling emotions more easily and more intensely.

Vulnerability to feeling emotional and developing emotional storms also increases for some with being tired, sick or hungry. Each of these states lends itself to increased stress and emotionality.

Others have a genetic predisposition to mental health conditions such as mood disorders (depression, Bipolar Disorder, anxiety). These people naturally have a heightened likelihood of experiencing certain emotions frequently or routinely, whether being treated or not. Coupled with stressful periods in life, intense emotions can be triggered.

A lack of knowledge, experience and skills

Difficulty with or struggle with emotions can also point to a lack of inner skills and resources to deal with them when they arise. As we develop, we naturally acquire skills to get us through life and understanding our emotions is no different. However, due to a range of factors, a person may miss out on learning about their emotions in a constructive, validating and practical way. We will explore this in later chapters. This book aims to provide practices or skills to assist in development of helpful approaches to emotional challenges, to address this gap in skills and knowledge.

A lack of confidence

If we haven't learnt about handling difficult, challenging emotions within us, we frequently do not have a positive experience in trying to do so. A deficit of skills, a lack of past experiences of successfully getting through an emotional storm, an ongoing hangover of unprocessed emotions from past painful or emotional events in life, can all mean that a person can end up feeling a significant lack of confidence around any emotions.

Emotions can then feel scary and deeply problematic—something to try and avoid at any cost when confidence in managing and surviving them is low. But of course, to avoid emotions is impossible ...

IN SUMMARY

Key areas are presented that tap into different aspects of having emotions and the everyday, lived experience of your emotional self. They are drawn from a wealth of personal and professional experience over many years and represent key messages that I repeatedly coach clients around in therapeutic work. They represent recurring, basic principles and practices that I utilise in my own emotional self-care personally and professionally.

These key areas naturally interlink and overlap in many respects. Each can be taken independently and are designed to be brought into your life—through increasing awareness and understanding of yourself and emotions; through practising strategies that assist with effective navigation or management of emotional states; through recognising and harnessing the rich benefits that emotions can bring to life.

As you apply practices to your own emotional experience and emotional self, the links between the keys will become apparent and can be used together naturally, providing a more evolved and sophisticated practice when challenging emotions arise.

Emotions can be likened to weather, and in particular storms, for the experience of being inundated and at the mercy of wild, intense elements. Some emotions are directly linked to our fight-or-flight system being activated. This book seeks to arm you with a range of practices and understanding, to support a shift in the way in which intense weather is prepared for and regarded.

On a personal level, through investigation and trial, practice and perseverance, I have moved from being a passenger on the SS Minow in the tropical storm, thrown about and shipwrecked on a random beach, to an equipped proactive storm chaser of the cyclone belt — resourced to better monitor the storm and manage risk as best as possible, and respecting the storm for its power and beauty.

While clearly acknowledging that emotions represent one aspect of ourselves and belong to a broader context of being alive and human, to shine a light on emotions as a topic of knowledge and contemplation, unto itself, is a demonstrated pathway to a greater capacity to effectively manage, understand and draw on the riches they offer.

TAKEAWAY PRACTICES

- Notice any emotions arising as you move through the day. Take the time to name them, using the list of emotions from earlier in the chapter to help you to be as accurate as possible. Note if you need to expand your emotion vocabulary to cover the variety of feelings you have.

- Pay attention in your life to when you may detect the fight-or-flight response activated through some of the signs listed in the chapter, such as through a feeling of stress, fear or physiological changes.

- During emotions take time to note any judgements coming in around the emotion being 'positive' or 'negative'. Simply observe this when it occurs and note which emotions are labelled in which way.

- When feeling an emotion, notice if you are also tired, hungry or sick. Acknowledge that this may increase emotionality and is a part of the context for you.

CHAPTER 2

The Relentless Flow

There is one basic truth about our emotions—no matter who you are, what you do, how you live your life or what you have (or don't have), emotions are part of the package deal of being human and alive.

There is no difference across class, economic status, nationality, age or gender, to having and living with emotions—you cannot buy or barter your way out of them. We are all basically the same in our core humanity, and this includes possessing an 'emotional self' and the capacity to feel. We all share the same biology including the brain and hormonal systems that kick into action as we move through life, facilitating the experience of emotional feeling. We all contain this same capacity and potential for felt emotion within, and of emotional expression without.

Equally, no matter what you may endeavour to do with your emotions and how you manage your emotional self—whatever philosophy, strategy, attitude, behaviour or approach you might take up to corral those wily feelings—the truth is that emotions will just keep on coming. They are a relentless river.

As long as we remain breathing and conscious, the flow of emotions will keep on. Seeking to resist, to escape or force them into submission, is therefore futile.

In a recent study, researchers Trampe, Quoidbach and Taquet sought to understand how frequently emotions occurred on a daily level. This type of study had not been undertaken previously, reflecting the lag in scientific interest and endeavour to specifically value and understand human emotion. Participants were asked to monitor and log their emotions as they arose throughout their day. Through examining the responses of over 11,000 people, across fifteen months, this study concluded that some form of emotion was felt for 90% of waking hours. This highlights how we *are* feeling beings and feeling is an essential part of the substance of our lives.

So, this first key to better understanding our feelings, particularly when they are strong, intense, overwhelming, irritating, inconvenient, challenging or uncomfortable, is recognising the natural truth and legitimacy of feeling.

It involves acceptance of emotion.

Why? Because … emotions just are.

KEY CONCEPT: Isness

Within Eastern spiritual practices the idea of 'Isness' emerged many centuries ago as spiritual and philosophical teachers reflected on and perceived the truth of life and the nature of the world we inhabit.

Isness means: The fact that a thing is, the quality or state of actual, objective existence or being.

This first key area requires a realistic, matter-of-fact view of the existence we inhabit, with emotions as an essential part of it. Emotions need to be dealt with one way or another simply because they are there and they will continue to be there, within ourselves and as part of our reality and responsiveness to the world we live in. Simply put, they exist and will prevail across the events of our lives, and the screen of our hearts and minds. And that is that.

ACCEPTANCE AND SURRENDER

This first key centres on the understanding of the 'isness' of emotions. And the 'how' of this first key is centred on a fundamental 'surrender' to having emotions.

Surrender means acknowledgement and acceptance of emotions being part of what to expect within ourselves as we move through life. Surrender and acceptance do not necessarily mean agreeing with the feelings or liking them.

For example, we can have great difficulty in accepting the pain of grief, or the fear of our boss, or the guilt around not pleasing others, but those kind of feelings commonly arise and simply represent how it is for you emotionally, at the time, with circumstances in life. Equally, someone experiencing depression or anxiety as a formal diagnosed mental health condition, may need to accept that they will feel emotional symptoms as part of their *isness* from time to time with their condition.

The benefits of surrendering or accepting emotions are important to explore as emotions actually serve a vital function in our life. They need to be there and there is benefit to them being there. Moreover, there is great benefit to being present with them when they arise and consciously allowing the emotions to have space to be.

BENEFITS OF OUR EMOTIONS

So, what do we have to gain from having our emotions? What do we gain if we surrender to them being a fact?

There are numerous benefits to having emotions and emotions serve purposes that are often grossly unappreciated. As noted in the study on emotions in everyday life, we live emotionally every single day, however, if you asked people what they are there for, many would struggle to know clearly and confidently why emotions are of value.

In years of therapeutic practice, I have constantly worked with people who entered counselling at a point of emotional turmoil. They have often felt confused, overwhelmed and in struggle with the emotions they are experiencing. Part of the work required, to create a genuine positive shift, is grounded in tuning into the emotions present, seeking to understand the context for them and their message. This helps access the value and meaning of the feeling, which then tends to unlock a shift from an inner storm to one of greater calmness, clarity and strength. And with this shift in understanding, capacity for acceptance expands.

THE FUNCTION OF EMOTIONS AND FEELING

Why be with our emotions?

Some main reasons that emotions are valuable to us and serve a purpose include:
- emotions provide a primary richness to living
- emotions are information
- emotions provide motivation.

EMOTIONS PROVIDE A PRIMARY RICHNESS TO LIVING

Firstly, emotions provide an unequivocal richness to life, as illustrated in the reflection point below.

REFLECTION POINT

Take a moment now and think of three of the most important events of your life. Stop reading and write down three significant moments …

Did you do it? If not, stop again and take the time to do this simple exercise. Look for three moments or events that have felt important to you from your life. Remember that we are all individuals and there is no right or wrong to strive for or to be concerned about. Take the freedom, as much as you can, to be open and honest with yourself around your emotional self and your lived experience.

Okay, so let's have a look.

How did you judge what was important? How did you weigh up your life and scan for significance?

Chances are that you might have chosen from two broad types of events:

- achieving or losing something of significance.
- an event or moment to do with a relationship with another person.

Achieving or losing something of significance

With the many people I have worked with over the years, a sense of accomplishment, of achievement and the building up of things in their life is incredibly meaningful to them. These types of things, in our Western-based society, include study and work as common types of achievement. Thinking from a survival system level, from our fight-or-flight mode, achievement can be deeply enmeshed with creating or attaining a more solid base of material security that allows us to lower our vigilance around survival—to move from survival mode to thriving or flourishing, attaining a more securely established base in life.

For many clients, these types of goals represent possibility for the future, financial security and prosperity, hope, a feeling of control and self-determination. Security also allows for greater choice and options being available.

I have had many clients who, while facing great challenges and pain in their current circumstances, cited their part-time study as the thread in their life of difference. It highlighted the life they were working towards—of positivity, growth, and hope. For those who made it to graduation, the sense of accomplishment was tangible. It also provided acknowledgement and esteem from others in their life. It contributed to a sense of self and identity that they valued.

Equally, for some people an important moment in their life might be the loss of something that was valuable. The death of someone close is a primary example. Examples of other critical losses can include one's health and independence, loss of community such as when people migrate including refugees, loss of innocence and a sense of safety when a traumatic or violent event occurs, loss of livelihood including businesses, family businesses and farms during drought or changes in industry.

An event or moment to do with a relationship to another person

The other main type of important and significant event involves connection with others. The type of feelings that contribute to significance include the experience of love, trust, attachment, understanding and commitment. Equally, significance can be about relationship challenges, crossing over into the previous category of loss.

When my father died from cancer, I was fourteen years old. It was only nine months from his diagnosis to his death, and my whole family was in shock for most of that time. To complicate matters, I was in boarding school and separated from much family contact.

Up until about the age of thirty, I would readily name his death as the moment of my life with most significance and weight. It dominated my life for a very long time, despite actively grappling with the profound feelings of loss and pain, and seeking to 'feel better', seeking to 'move on with my life'. Scanning the word list from the previous chapter, the words *bereft* or *aggrieved* summed up my dominant emotional experience. That was my reality—my emotional *isness*—even though I desperately wanted to be free of it. Translating it into storm analogies, it was akin to that type of thunderstorm off in the distance, constantly rumbling; sometimes softer, sometimes seemingly moving closer and becoming louder. Grumble, grumble, grumble.

When we think about relationships in our life and relating in general, emotions form the primary substance of how we experience these connections. I think of our emotions as a kind of 'superhighway' of connection with others. Our feelings guide us, motivate us and keep us in relationships, forming a primary binding medium for connection. Alternately, they also let us know when we do not feel right in a relationship.

... So, what is the point of recalling three significant important moments? It serves to highlight how emotions are an essential part of every valuable, memorable moment of life. What makes moments in life memorable is the emotional value elicited and the ongoing emotional association that it holds when recalled.

Meaning is imbued with emotional value; memory is usually imbued with feelings. In fact, we could declare that meaning is actually defined by the emotional value felt.

In weighing up significance and importance in our lives we usually go for times when emotions were generated. These emotions may be of reward, celebration, love, triumph and reckoning. They might be of grief, pain and sadness in losing someone or something we loved dearly.

In our complex nervous system and neurobiology, the limbic system is a key part of the brain that facilitates emotional experience and simultaneously, facilitates the laying down and accessing of our memories. Many years after an actual event, when we recall it, the memory can trigger emotions from that time, that become alive and present once more in the current moment.

EMOTIONS ARE INFORMATION

A second value of having emotions is that they give us information about ourselves in our environment, and in our life. Emotions provide an immediate feedback system for us around our current situation, environment, or about ourselves. This is tied in with our fight-or-flight system as described earlier, in responding to threats we may perceive through our senses.

Over the years I have worked with innumerable clients who have experienced abusive behaviour at the hands of other people.

Commonly, various types of abuse occurred within relationships that were meant to be safe, loving and protective. This kind of betrayal and hurt constitutes a very prevalent type of trauma that is recognised alongside single-event accidents, war experiences and violence by strangers.

The sense of danger that people are left with, the activation of the nervous system through the fight-or-flight mechanism, are healthy responses in the face of danger. When I point this out to clients—that the uncomfortable, intense emotions are actually healthy, protective responses to traumatic events—they often suddenly have a different view of the emotions they feel so troubled by. They are validated in feeling upset, distressed, angry, shocked or bereaved.

We need to learn to understand and speak the language of our emotions in terms of the information they give us, or we risk missing their intrinsic value, and the flow on benefits emotions offer.

The information that emotions provide us is important and matters. Emotions provide a vital guide to assessing our circumstances.

EMOTIONS PROVIDE MOTIVATION

A third benefit of having emotions is that our feelings—whether felt as comfortable and rewarding, painful and uncomfortable—often provide a driving force for motivating us into action that ultimately benefits our life.

I had a client who had been extremely close to her grandmother since childhood. Her grandmother had provided a sense of love, stability and positive feelings that no-one else in her family had come close to. In fact, within the rest of the family there was a significant amount of conflict and tension. As an adult with her own children, this client's grief at losing her grandmother was significantly compounded by the behaviour of the rest of the family after the death. They cremated her grandmother with no notice and without any kind of funeral or memorial service. My client naturally felt angry and robbed of honouring and saying goodbye to her beloved grandmother. Many aspects of this whole experience created additional pain for this client, compounding her grief. She felt stuck with these painful feelings because she could not change what had happened.

In therapy, with exploration of this situation, the client was amazed to hear of the option to create her own ritual to still say goodbye. She had not realised that she could in fact do this for herself despite what had occurred with the rest of the family. Subsequently, she held a farewell ritual at the graveside with her young children participating. Through this she was able to restore a sense of rightness in her world and address the difficult emotions she had been experiencing.

The pain and anger this client had felt at the way others in her family had behaved with the passing of her grandmother, was extremely important information for her and motivated her into action with what was within her control, for herself. She needed to be able to say goodbye, she needed the assistance that funeral rites offer people to process loss. The challenging emotions provided information and motivation to act, tapping into options available to her, to attend to her emotional needs.

THE NATURE OF EMOTIONS

Across many centuries, emotions have been symbolised by water and weather. These metaphors or symbols lend themselves to three qualities of emotions that help increase understanding of their nature.

1) The quality of flow

The word *flow* describes an action or movement. Flow is natural movement seen across many aspects of life. If we think about bodies of water such as the ocean, rivers, waves on lakes, if we think about the growth of trees and foliage in nature, if we think about our own physical bodies and the movement of breath, the blood circulating as the heart pumps, movement is present and characterises an essential part of much of nature and life.

Movement is a critical constant feature of all of these. The word *emotion* comes from the Latin word *movere*, meaning to move, with the word *emotion* being formed from e-motion—to be 'in motion'. Weather flows. Water flows. Emotions flow.

2) The quality of relentlessness or 'eternal flow'

Relentlessness means persistent and continuous. We need to accept that feelings are part of being alive and will be present in our lives as part of the very core of aliveness itself. Emotions, like a relentless river, will just keep flowing because flowing is their nature. Emotions like weather will continue to be. Emotions will continue to come and go as long as we are alive and breathing. We are destined to feel just as we are destined to always have weather in some form.

3) The quality of changeability

Water changes its flow according to conditions. Conditions can be the terrain the water is flowing in or the other conditions such as the source of water, wind and temperature. And of course, conditions can alter and change. Likewise, our emotions can change in response to circumstances and events.

Emotions are a response or reaction to the rest of the world we live in and events within us. It is natural that they change. Sometimes we see the changes coming and sometimes they take us by surprise ... However, changeability is a core part of the nature of emotions.

Interference with flow

By noting the qualities of water and weather, we can also see how going against the flow, fighting what is—the *isness* of the nature of something— can lead to exhaustion, frustration, pain and defeat. As we can observe in the natural world barriers to flow, so can we observe in ourselves barriers to the flow of our emotions when they arise.

From a young age I remember some of my earliest life lessons involved safety around water. There was danger to be had and respect to be given to water in all its forms: the ocean, the local community pool and the bathtub.

Growing up in a country of sport and water lovers, I learnt early on about what to do if I got caught in a strong current or 'rip' while swimming in the ocean. When caught in such a strong current carrying a swimmer away from the shoreline, the fight-or-flight system kicks in naturally (and appropriately). The urge of the swimmer is to get back to the shore, and out of the grip of the current. People will naturally try to swim towards where they want to be—the shore and solid ground—and thus try to swim directly against the current.

The force of the current is usually stronger than the person's physical strength and stamina. People exhaust themselves fighting the flow, swimming head-on against the current in what becomes a fight for their life. Yet paradoxically, this urge increases the risk of drowning as they lose the energy to keep their head above water. The direct fight with the flow depletes them and achieves little. Instead, it significantly raises the danger faced.

Safety organisations, such as Surf Life Saving Australia, suggest the key to handling this situation is not to fight the current directly but to go with the flow by floating, using the energy of the current to actually assist you and allow it to return you to shore, such as on a wave. A second strategy is to gently move sideways across the force of the water current, eventually delivering you out of the rip, with moderate, achievable effort. Both are shown in the diagram below.

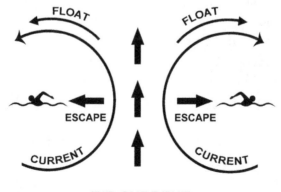

RIP CURRENT

Intense emotions and strong water currents are similar. To resist is futile, and it is precisely this resistance that exhausts us, creates bigger issues and fuels further challenges. The flow of the emotions needs to be accepted and respected in the way we address them within.

Barriers to flow and our fight-or-flight system

Emotions can be a source of stress and tension, and can absorb much of our energy in seeking to navigate them. They can arise at times when we already have too much on our plate—or when we least expect it, seemingly derailing all well-thought out plans, and adding a dimension of challenge to getting on with life. This is the point where resistance to emotions being a valid part of life can kick in.

Over the years as I have worked with many people during times of intense feelings, and I would be a rich woman if I had a dollar for every client I have helped *not* resist their emotions, as uncomfortable and painful as they were.

We inadvertently, unconsciously, resist intensity and pain.

It makes sense when we consider how we have evolved and the need for survival, the way in which the fight-or-flight system operates. We evolved to naturally fight pain or any perception of discomfort, as part of our much-needed survival system. We naturally want to feel comfortable and safe.

Some common ways of resisting our emotions when we fear their intensity can include the following:

- avoiding the feelings by refusing to talk about them or acknowledge them
- distracting from the feelings by strategies such as keeping busy, filling our time and space with all sorts of things
- denying the feelings by refusing to admit to ourselves or others the truth of what we may feel
- using addictive or compulsive behaviours to resist the emotional truth (often pain) through substances (alcohol, prescription or illicit drugs, food, tobacco) or behaviours (shopping, gambling, exercise, stealing, sex, overworking)

- fighting the feelings as if they should not be there and need a strong defence
- judging the feelings as if they are a sign of something being wrong, something to be ashamed of, a sign of weakness or craziness.

Other barriers may be less driven by ourselves, but nevertheless are a barrier to being with emotions:
- lack of skills to be with the emotions
- lack of safety in life to allow the truth of our feelings to surface
- lack of insight into what is needed to feel emotions unimpeded.

REFLECTION POINT

Do you relate to any of these barriers to allowing and accepting your emotions?

Take some time to write about any attitudes or strategies you identify as inner barriers to emotions.

The next time a feeling arises note any resistance to it.

BEING WITH EMOTIONS

To help with our ability to be with our emotions, to be with their *isness*—to accept and surrender to them as an essential part of being alive—awareness of barriers to flow is helpful.

The 'how' of this awareness is by practising being alert, aware and mindful of what is.

KEY CONCEPT: Mindfulness

Mindfulness as a practice is increasingly used in psychology due to its helpfulness across many different types of challenges with mental wellbeing and emotional health. Originating in different forms in Eastern philosophy and spiritual practice, it was brought into Western psychology and culture during the 1960s and 70s. Further research and development of contemporary practices has made it an increasingly common and popular strategy for treatment in mental health.

Having spent twelve years living in a meditation centre in India, I was very excited when I embarked on my studies in mental health and counselling that under the term 'mindfulness' this approach had become recognised and acknowledged for its benefits to emotional and psychological health.

So, what is mindfulness?

Mindfulness means paying attention, shifting your awareness or consciousness to the present moment with everything that is there, and without judgement of what is.

In a nutshell, mindfulness is:
- paying attention
- in the present moment
- without judgement.

For me, right now, as I write this paragraph mindfully, the present moment is sitting here in my local café, with my computer, tapping on the keyboard, with the words I am typing going through my mind each moment as I write. Simultaneously, I am aware of sounds outside of the café including the traffic on the wet road. I am aware of the sounds of voices and music in the café. I am aware of a feeling of mild contentment present as I achieve my writing goals. I am aware of feeling safe and at home in my familiar local café environment.

Right now, what are you aware of when you shift your attention into the present moment?

PRACTICE POINT: Open Mindfulness of the Moment

Pause for a moment and see what you notice. Allow whatever is there for you right now without seeking to avoid anything or make anything different. Take a minute to be present in the way I have described. Pause from reading and practise being mindful of this moment ...

Okay, so coming back ...

When we are aware, alert and conscious to the present moment, a number of things can be noted as present in our field of awareness simultaneously.

Below is a list of many of the common things that you might find in your present moment to note and be aware of:
- where you physically are (environment)
- your body (aches, sensations, the position you are in, breathing, tensions)
- sounds (external sounds close and distant, internal body sounds such as your pulse or tinnitus)
- thoughts including verbal words or self-talk, images, memories, judgements
- emotions or feelings.

Being mindful makes us practise being present to what *is* and frequently what is includes emotions. Presence—the act of simply being aware—to our emotions is extremely powerful. It is often missing as we may unconsciously react to strong feelings and go into an automatic mode of seeking to handle or avoid them. Or be overwhelmed by them. It also helps us become aware of any automatic beliefs and thoughts that enter the relentless cascade of activity when uncomfortable emotions arise, when the fight-or-flight system gets activated.

KEY CONCEPT: Cognition

Cognition refers to mental processes facilitated by the brain and nervous system. It includes thoughts, use of language, memories, imagination, visualisation, information processing and analysis, learning, attention and perception. Cognitions can be both conscious and unconscious, incorporating consciousness itself. Cognitions are often associated with and connected to emotional experience, as is explored throughout this book.

KEY CONCEPT: Validation

Validation and the capacity to be able to validate feelings is an important factor in the process of having an emotion and minimising emotional storms. The issue of validation usually plays a major role in why people may struggle with their emotions. It therefore offers a key opportunity to improve the way we approach and handle emotions, intense or mild. We can validate our own feelings, as well as other people's.

To validate our emotions means:
- to acknowledge the feeling exists
- to show understanding that the feeling is being experienced
- to express acceptance of the emotion being experienced.

A way of doing this with myself is to say internally or aloud, 'Right now I feel … (sad, angry, excited, overwhelmed, etc.)'. With other people it might mean saying, 'I see/hear/understand that right now you feel … (sad, angry, excited, overwhelmed, etc.)'.

With both yourself and others, validating means to give space to the feeling by acknowledging and showing understanding, together with not questioning the internal experience or judging, dismissing, avoiding or minimising it. This is the definition of being mindful. Mindfulness offers the major strategy for being with our emotions in a healthy, effective and validating way.

A common factor that can complicate and intensify the emotional experience, is that the person having the emotion feels that the emotion is not valid—the feelings are wrong, stupid, embarrassing, inappropriate, signs of weakness or not acceptable. Invalidating our emotions is built on judgement of them, on questioning their existence and legitimacy.

These type of invalidating ideas and judgements can be received from our environment and people around us, for a variety of reasons (which will be explored in subsequent chapters). But we also inevitably fail to validate ourselves, often absorbing messages received from outside us and then internalising them and running them from within. Not validating your own emotions involves judging them. Often, we have never learned how to validate our feelings.

The keys presented in this book aim to support increased emotional understanding and effective navigation of our emotional lives, so we can benefit from their messages more often. This strategy rests on the basis that *all* emotions are valid. It relates back to accepting the isness of emotions as part of being human and alive. It is a *valid* part of the human experience and entering a debate with yourself or others about an emotion being right or wrong (which essentially is what the whole 'validity debate' is about) is not necessary.

All emotions are valid, and this also relates back to the principle that there is no right or wrong around emotions, they just are. Isness always prevails.

IN SUMMARY

Emotions are part of being alive and human, and emotional experiences will keep occurring as part of this, endlessly. The nature of emotions can be likened to innate qualities of weather and water. Awareness can help us identify barriers to feelings flowing within.

Practising being mindful to our emotional self, our emotional reality, can bring increased acceptance, willingness and acknowledgement of the experience of emotions as valid, to our reality. Mindfulness represents a straightforward awareness of what is present, without seeking to adjust it in any way.

TAKEAWAY PRACTICES

- Practise **Open Mindfulness of the Moment** during the day for five minutes or more.

- Practise mindfulness of your emotions when they arise. Note the qualities of water and weather (flow, relentlessness and changeability) of your emotions when they come during your day.

- Find flowing water such as the ocean, a creek or river, or water flowing in a fountain. Watch or listen to it mindfully for five minutes or more. Notice the qualities of the water that help remind you of the qualities of emotions.

- Notice any barriers to your emotions flowing during your day, including judging emotions and not validating them.

- Notice when an emotion arises if there are any cognitions or thoughts connected to the feeling. This may include certain thoughts, memories, ideas, beliefs or judgements.

CHAPTER 3

Mind the Gap

Experiencing an emotion is a process—a process in time, with multiple, multidimensional aspects and stages to it. However, it is not a rigid, fixed kind of process. How it is experienced varies greatly, depending on the person, situation, circumstance and type of emotion. Yet, the bottom line is that a process occurs with the stirring of emotions whether fast, slow, in-between, quietly or loudly. There is a time-embedded process to all emotions arising and passing. And there are also shared markers or parts to the feeling process that we can get familiar with.

The gap is not empty

For many people there can be a 'gap' in their awareness—or what they are conscious of—during an emotion. Sometimes this gap is brief and quick, giving the sense of it occurring in a bit of a blur and being suddenly 'hijacked' by the emotion. Sometimes the process lasts for days or even weeks without having clarity about what is happening. That is the point at which people will state the emotional storm kicked in and 'hijacked' them. It is precisely this 'in-between' gap in our awareness where shining a light in, to see what is actually occurring, can be incredibly helpful.

… Because … (drum roll) … the gap is not empty.

There *is* a process that has its own logical flow and order, that we may simply not be aware of or familiar with. We may never have been prompted to notice this emotional process or guided around it. We do not know what there is to know and what markers to look out for. We do not know how to sense, approach or name the events we are feeling. Remedying this and creating a significant difference in the experience of having emotions can be as simple as minding the gap, or paying attention.

Minding the gap—identifying the process and exploring ways to be with it—is the focus of this key.

BENEFITS OF PAYING ATTENTION TO THE EMOTIONAL PROCESS

Becoming acquainted with the process helps in several ways, by:

Holding a realistic perspective versus a distorted one

Viewing the reality of the emotional process versus having the experience of an emotion overtake you in a rush, creates a very different sense of the whole experience. When we see what is occurring, it provides a more accurate, graspable and meaningful process. We are in touch with reality versus holding a distorted, inaccurate interpretation of the emotional experience. We can then reduce misinterpretation of sensations and cognitions, and bring consciousness to how we respond versus unconsciously reacting.

Reassurance during the emotion

By seeing the process involved in having an emotion, the potential for further emotional alarm reduces. As part of our response to perceptions of threat, we seek control. Having emotions can often feel

38

like a loss of control and this compounds the emotions, with fear or anxiety increasing, along with a sense of a lack of power, influence or understanding. Having a more accurate understanding, helps us find our bearings during an intense feeling, which can markedly reduce the potential for further emotions being triggered. Seeing emotions more clearly provides reassurance.

Being with the process as it occurs

A familiarity with and building up of accurate emotional knowledge, assists us in staying with the process. In the spirit of the first key area, the acceptance of emotions and staying with reality is infinitely rewarding. It provides us with a better opportunity to respond to emotions in a helpful way.

Seeing that there is an actual process occurring versus a blurred unclear experience, helps restore some sense of order and perspective. Concrete features or 'markers' are discovered to be there, to be noticed. It can also assist in a feeling of slowing the process down, so that the sense of being hit by a storm, in a rush, is reduced.

Reduces unhelpful, compounding reactions

Respecting the process helps us unhinge from judgements, pressures and automatic interpretations that arise when we have an emotion, that we may place on ourselves or feel from external sources.

Not acknowledging the process means that all sorts of other unrealistic, pressuring, judgemental and ill-informed responses to emotion can dominate within. These come in as a way of trying to cope, but are often unhelpful because they are ill-informed. These meanings and interpretations, as well as secondary emotions, will be looked at later in the chapter.

Increases self-understanding

When in an emotion, having a working approach to the process, provides an opportunity to understand ourselves and our way of operating. Self-understanding can highlight certain patterns unique to our emotional selves.

For example:

- Do we tend to feel certain emotions more than others?
- Are we sensitive to certain triggers and circumstances?
- When we feel a certain emotion does it throw up memories from the past?
- Are some types of emotions more difficult for us to allow and be with than others?

Self-understanding of our emotional selves can highlight repeated patterns in our thinking, or cognitions, including beliefs we may carry about ourselves that accompany the emotion. The ongoing impact of life experiences may be revealed, and this can play a significant role in understanding ourselves. This will be explored more fully in the later chapters (including emotional habits and the effects of personal history).

In building self-understanding, we boost the capacity to manage challenges and navigate emotions because we understand better our vulnerabilities and strengths.

UNDERSTANDING THE PROCESS

The gap is part of the common experience

As human beings who have a fight-or-flight system (our own inbuilt survival mechanism) we like certainty. Our system is primed to seek out clear positions and clarity of the experience within ourselves and in the world we inhabit, to allow our need for vigilance to relax. Safety and the removal of any perceived threat is our first and foremost biological and psychological need.

The 'in-between' stage, where something has changed or ended, and the new has not yet arrived or unfolded, where we sit in insecurity and a state of 'not-knowing,' can therefore play havoc with us. It can activate our fight-or-flight system. Yet, such gaps and stages of 'not knowing' are incredibly common in life. These stages usually involve waiting for a process to take place or unfold; for a new order, consequences, or an adjustment to occur that we can then identify and name clearly. Examples of common life gaps include:

- changes around health
- waiting to hear about a job interview
- changes around life satisfaction or fulfillment
- changes in our community or social network
- needing to move to a new house but not knowing where you will move yet
- a conflict with someone who matters to you that is not yet resolved
- someone behaving differently to their normal selves and not yet knowing why or what it may mean.

Such uncertainties can activate alarm and stress within, thus making us more vulnerable to the feelings associated with being in a fight-or-flight response: fear, impatience, panic, anger or pain.

Emotional experiences themselves can similarly feel like being in a gap, with a period of not knowing what we are feeling or quite why until the process is nearing completion. Closer to completion, we can then identify what we felt, grounding it in understanding and a perspective or context within our life that makes sense to us. With our emotions, hindsight is certainly a valuable thing.

PAYING ATTENTION

When we pay attention to something, we already instigate change. Awareness immediately creates a qualitative difference to our inner experience; presence to our emotions is powerful. So, within this key, we bring our practice of mindfulness.

To recap, mindfulness means to pay attention to the present moment, without judgement. We now bring mindfulness to the process of having an emotion.

THE EMOTION PROCESS

Understanding process

The process we tune into is the movement of the feeling—the flow of stages that might typically make up having an emotion, as it occurs within.

Process can be defined as:

- a phenomenon marked by gradual changes that leads to a particular result
- a series of actions or operations taken to achieve an end.

We are tapping into the natural flow of feelings as likened to the flow and movement of water in the last chapter.

So, what occurs during the process of having an emotion?

This has been explored in various therapeutic approaches such as Cognitive Behavioural Therapy (CBT) and Dialectical Behavioural Therapy (DBT). I have drawn elements from both, married with experience of watching my own emotional processes and that of clients.

The diagram below provides an overview of elements, in a sequence typical of the emotion process. These are the moving parts that we

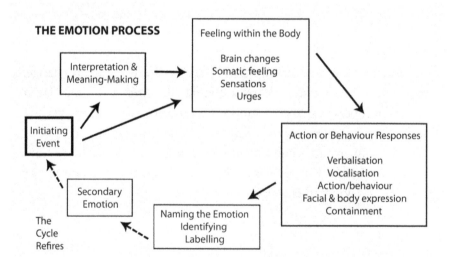

can bring awareness to, observe, and note during feeling. As with all processes, there may be variation and what is presented represents a general guide.

THE MOVING PARTS OF THE EMOTIONAL PROCESS

Initiating event

There is a moment where the emotion begins, usually marked by an event. We call this the initiating event of the emotion, or the triggering event.

Events that can create an emotional response, a process, vary widely from person to person. There is no right or wrong; there simply is the fact that an event has activated an emotion within you.

Examples of initiating events and triggers include:
- a memory
- an illness
- a worry
- a realisation or recognition
- an interaction with another person
- getting a shock or surprise
- an accident or near miss
- a change in circumstances
- a loss or disappointment
- added stress or demand upon you
- dynamics within a relationship (personal, work, family, a friend, a stranger, an authority).

As can be seen, some events are easily identified as triggers or initiating events of emotions. They are relatable and easily understood—almost, we could say, seen to be emotion-worthy. There is a shared empathy and recognition amongst yourself and other people that something occurred that has stirred feelings up.

Examples of easily recognisable events and the feelings initiated could include:

- a reaction prompted by a surprise party—a mixture of shock and surprise and joy could be common
- a break-up of an intimate relationship could be a source of feelings of sadness, anger or overwhelm
- the death of a loved one, a significant illness or loss, could trigger emotions such as sadness, grief, fear and anger.

However, more subtle, even invisible triggers and initiating events—private to yourself and not necessarily obvious to other people—can equally create emotions.

Examples of these include:

- a dream
- a memory
- a thought
- a secret recalled
- a sensitivity being triggered relating to personal history.

REFLECTION POINT

Think of a recent time where you identify having had an emotion arise. In hindsight (a wonderful thing!), seek to identify what event initiated or triggered the emotion.

Meaning or interpretation

At this point, after an initiating event, our mind can kick in, in a rapid, automatic way. The mind offers words and ideas to try to make sense of the trigger, to interpret the phenomenon being experienced and to assess the situation.

The meaning or interpretation that occurs comes through our cognitive processes and is where we often apply language to the sensory information we are receiving.

Such cognitions may be identified as any of the following:
- judgements
- beliefs
- memories
- opinions
- labelling or naming
- commentary
- analysis.

Interpretation is the inner cognitive process of making sense of, and deriving meaning, of the event. This meaning-making and interpretation can be coloured by our personal 'frame of reference'. This frame of reference is made up of past experiences, catalogued within our memory, which continuously shape our responses to life now. Such experience helps inform us of the kind of consequences that could happen from an event. It is natural and frequently helpful to draw on prior life experience.

However, it can intensify emotions or make us jump to conclusions, particularly if our fight-or-flight system is activated. In turn, these past experiences can also crystallise into beliefs that we apply to ourselves. They may be accurate or inaccurate, or half true. We will look at this aspect of the past colouring current experience in the next chapter.

As part of the interpretation and meaning we ascribe to the initiating event, beliefs about ourselves that seem relevant can be evoked. For example, if the initiating event occurs in relation to another person, beliefs might kick in such as: 'I am going to be rejected again', 'No-one likes me', 'I always look stupid in front of people', 'I make people angry', or 'I am not good at relating'.

These interpretations can occur immediately after the triggering event and contribute to the subsequent feeling response or may occur simultaneously with the actual feeling response.

Either way, the interpretation can be a critical and complex part of the process that occurs, and the overall intensity and course of the process can much depend on the interpretation or meaning we arrive at.

REFLECTION POINT

Think of a recent time where you identified having an emotion arise. In hindsight, seek to identify what thoughts occurred after the initiating event in relation to it. There may be multiple thoughts.

What meaning did you make of the triggering event?

Was this interpretation a belief or a judgement? Was there a memory or association with your past?

The feeling within the body

Emotions usually have a somatic or bodily experience to them, a sensation or sensations that alert you to having an emotional feeling. It can be experienced as a kind of bodily stirring.

These physical sensations represent changes in your brain, including chemical and electrical responses to the triggering event, that in turn affect other parts of the body, through their effects. Emotions can have a significant bodily, physical aspect to them, that brings into play blood circulation and the muscles, the digestive system, and of course all the nerves running through our body. This creates change within the face and body. Importantly, such changes also can initiate noticeable shifts in breathing when we are emotional.

As a child who often felt overwhelmed and anxious by new things, I recall getting pins and needles in the bottom of my feet when about to go into an unfamiliar situation like a school camp. It made me 'antsy' and uncomfortable. In hindsight, I now recognise my fight-or-flight system engaging in those moments, with the readiness to move fast or escape. It was frequently accompanied by wanting to go to the toilet (the evacuation response preparing me to act swiftly) and worry thoughts (the mental processes focusing in on the most threatening aspects and possibilities in readiness to respond).

The sense of overwhelm often created further discomfort and I had no perspective to put this experience in, except knowing that I did not like it.

It was only later in adult life I came to appreciate the normalcy of these feelings when facing new situations outside my comfort zone. I am now better at identifying my emotions and understanding that fear is often accompanied simultaneously by excitement in facing new and unknown situations. To this day such circumstances create physical tingling in my feet and tummy as the feelings of nervousness and excitement begin.

This aspect of the emotion process allows you to get to know your body better in how it responds, as well as your emotional process.

REFLECTION POINT

Think of a recent time where you identified having an emotion arise. Seek to identify how the emotion felt in your body. This part of the process can be much more accessible in the actual moment of the feeling but see what you recall in hindsight.

Note if the emotion was mainly located in one part of your body in particular—where does the emotion 'sit' in your body?

Note if certain feelings bring particular body sensations for you.

Action or behaviour impulses

When having an emotion, it is usually accompanied by an impulse to act. Emotions trigger action impulses. The action seeks to address the circumstance that stirred the emotion through prompting action, or launching into a behaviour. This may be to express the feeling outwardly as a communication to others vocally or verbally; expressing the feeling outwardly as a way of releasing some of the feeling intensity; it can be fleeing, freezing or fighting; it can be moving closer and embracing, jumping for joy; or collapsing in overwhelm or tears or relief, depending on the feeling and the action urge it prompts.

There are common action urges with certain emotions. With overwhelm, sadness, pain or embarrassment, there might come the impulse to cry, and to retreat or move away from something. With anger or frustration, the urge might be to fight (possibly in the spirit of fighting back), make verbal noise towards someone else, and to attack the perceived source of the stress or threat in some form.

With emotions such as happiness, joy and love, the action urge can be to verbalise, make noises of celebration or excitement and move towards others involved in the experience, sharing the moment. It can create a desire for connection with others and sharing of the feeling. With excitement, as I experienced as a child facing new things, it can include restlessness and agitation.

Below are some typical action responses to different emotions:

Emotion	Action or behaviour urge
Love	Move closer, approach the loved one
Joy	Smile, laugh, approach others, desire to share
Fear	Scream, run away, escape, flee, freeze, hide
Shame	Hide, retreat, avoid others, cry
Sadness	Cry, isolate, collapse, seek comfort
Anger	Fight, attack, intimidate, stand up to, hold ground.

These urges to act—the action or behaviour impulses—occur at a very fundamental, primal level of being. They often involve the fight-or-flight system and the action urge is usually aligned with reducing the stress of the emotional experience, whether it be desirable or undesirable. People can have different impulses depending upon other mediating factors such as upbringing, culture and temperament. This will be explored in the next chapter.

Action or behavioural impulses may be acted upon or not (as will be explored later in the chapter).

Naming or identifying the emotion

At this point—after the initiating event, the interpretation and meaning ascribed and the body feeling and action or behavioural impulses—naming or identifying the emotion is most possible. To identify the emotion and give it a name or label is an important part of developing greater understanding and building our ability to be with our emotions in an effective way. The emotion list in the first chapter is useful at this stage to help identify and name the feeling as accurately as possible.

The experience and movement of the emotion in the previous stages provides information and allows us to fully recognise the emotion being felt. The lapse in time and the process up until this point is what can seem like a blur or gap. To stay with this process often relies on staying with 'not knowing', insecurity and lack of clarity. We like to know where we stand and to be free of the tension of being 'in between' matters, yet the reality of the process contains stages of feeling without yet being clear.

From a mindfulness perspective, naming and identifying the emotion assists in seeing them with some observing distance; being able to take a step back within us, to more clearly recognise the experience.

Identifying the emotion serves to remove our own identification with it. Instead of stating 'I am angry', we can more accurately say, 'I am experiencing the feeling of anger' or 'I am experiencing anger right now'. This implies recognising that it is indeed a feeling state rather than us as a person.

REFLECTION POINT

Recall an experience where you went through an emotion and take the time to get clear and specific about what emotion it was. Use the list of emotions in Chapter 1 to assist you in considering the most accurate emotion name.

KEY CONCEPT: Secondary Emotions

When we have an emotional response to a triggering or initiating event, one of the common occurrences within, can be to have a **secondary emotional response** to the original emotion (the primary or core emotion) as shown in the diagram.

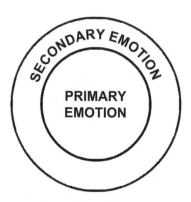

The actions, behaviours and expressions that flow from the primary or original emotion, may also in themselves trigger new emotions, thus initiating a new round of the loop of an emotional process. This is sometimes called 'metaemotion', meaning feelings about our feelings. It is a common phenomenon.

Becoming alert to and aware of any secondary emotions occurring is critical to understanding development of intense, stormy emotions, as it compounds, fuels and complicates the state of emotion considerably.

Some examples of secondary feeling reactions to primary or core feelings are:

- feeling angry at feeling upset and crying
- feeling anxious about feeling grief and crying
- feeling irritated with feeling fearful and wanting to escape
- feeling distressed when feeling frustrated and stuck
- feeling angry about feeling jealous and envious
- feeling guilty about feeling proud
- feeling ashamed about feeling happy
- feeling hopeless about feeling lonely.

As you can see from the examples, there can be a broad range of secondary feelings in reaction to the primary, core feeling.

REFLECTION POINT

Recall a time when you had an emotion arise. Note if a feeling about the feeling (a secondary emotional reaction) occurred. Notice if you have any emotions that you judged and explore where the judgement elicits a secondary feeling such as in the examples provided.

PRACTICE POINT: Map it Out

When you have an emotional experience take time to identify and write down each of the parts of the process.

Use the diagram of the emotion process to guide you and note the following from your own experience:
- identify the initiating event
- identify any interpretation or meaning
- identify any feeling in the body
- note any behaviour or action impulses
- name or identify the emotion
- was there a secondary emotion triggered?
- go through whole process for the secondary emotion too.

Initially, looking back in hindsight at a recent time where emotion came, can be easier to map out. However, with practice, this process can be applied at the time of the emotion to enhance clarity and self-understanding.

KEY CONCEPT: Expression and Containment

During the process outlined, the impulse to express the emotion frequently arises. This **expression** can be part of the action urge and at times of strongly felt emotion seems to occur without a choice. For example, in distress and fear, crying may occur as something that happens and not an outright action taken by you.

Crying often gives a sense of relief but also expresses to others around us how we are feeling. Facial expression can involuntarily express our feelings without us making it happen or being conscious of it happening.

Despite how we are feeling, it can take conscious awareness and another part of our mind to not express our emotions in an automatic way. With awareness, we can capture the moment as it occurs and while feeling the emotions, 'contain' the outward expression of this feeling.

Containment means to literally contain the feeling within us, to be able to hold feelings within, without their flowing outward into expression of any sort. For many people, including myself, such seeming control of emotional expression felt impossible for a long time. The idea of containing my emotions felt too much like having to supress them, or pushing them down because there was something wrong with them in the first place. The concept and practice of containment is definitely not akin to suppressing or bottling up the feelings or invalidating them. Why? Because we *consciously* contain, we judge the need and benefit for our self to give boundaries to our feelings, despite very much feeling them and validating what is happening emotionally within.

There can be good reasons to practice containing emotions. It is a mature stance we can take with ourselves when we are able, for reasons such as:

- It is not a safe environment to show our emotions. The response we may get is likely to be judgemental, lacking care or understanding
- It may be a place such as work where showing emotions may be unusual, regarded as inappropriate or unprofessional
- We need to be able to continue to do something or complete a function or task or role we are in

- We may want and need more private time to process the feeling, make meaning of it and consider the action or expression we might take
- A lack of clarity about what is happening as the emotion has come unexpectedly
- Containing the emotion within helps self-care by not reacting unconsciously
- Containment helps build self-respect and a sense of choice and control over or increased management of our emotional experiences
- Communication can be more cohesive and effective when not in strong emotion
- Communication about an important matter can be received better by others when not delivered with heightened emotion.

Emotional expression and containment can both be utilised in healthy and unhealthy ways. They can be overused or underused habitually. The ideal is to be able to do both at times where you assess the appropriateness of each; to have flexibility and respond in this moment, to this particular situation, versus a default way of operating emotionally.

Expression can be damaging to relationships and your reputation if you say things at the height of emotion that you would not normally say.

REFLECTION POINT

Notice if you have a tendency to express your feelings or hold them in. Using one versus choosing between the two may be due to lack of awareness and skills. If you notice a tendency towards one, experiment with the following opposite practice point when you have an opportunity. Both expression and containment involve validation and acknowledgement of the emotion, and each have an important place in management and navigation of our emotional selves.

PRACTICE POINT: Practising Containment

Expression of every emotion that arises can occur due to not being able to contain the feelings and validate them within.

Next time you become aware that you are in an emotion, exercise the inner skill of containment:
- acknowledge the feeling within that you are aware of
- hold the feeling within you
- feel your body like a vessel or container
- breath into the feeling gently
- through self-talk validate the feeling while containing it. 'Right now, I am feeling ...'

Note how hard it is for you not to act on the behaviour or action urge.

Extra supports can assist with developing the capacity to contain the emotion, including:
- moving your body through taking a walk or similar activity
- taking timeout from a situation that contributes to the emotion
- practise grounding or other mindfulness practices (see the later chapter on grounding).

PRACTICE POINT: Practising Expression

Overuse of containment may be due to not knowing how to express emotions. It can also be related to discomfort with the vulnerability that comes when feelings flow to the surface of our bodies and are visible to others. It may be due to a lack of practice or experience in expressing emotions.

The following ideas offer ways to begin to explore expression safely:
- acknowledge the feeling within that you are aware of
- use **the emotion process** to assist with describing what is going on inside you when you have a feeling, to support effective expression through words

- experiment with allowing emotion to show in your face and body when you are aware of it—literally breathing gently and inviting the emotion to the surface of your body.

SURFING THE EMOTION WAVE

Emotions tend to rise and fall, like a wave in the ocean—building momentum and intensity, rising to a peak, and then slowly subsiding as the wave crest turns and dissipates, as shown in the diagram.

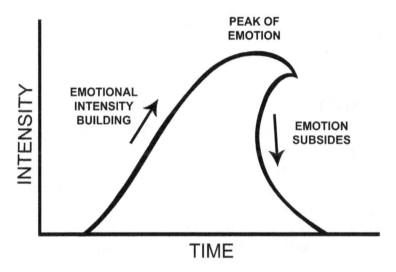

SURFING THE EMOTION WAVE

The practice of surfing the emotion wave offers a particular mindfulness-based practice of containment. While having impulses and urges, we learn we do not need to act on them, but instead observe the experience of this wave of emotion within.

Derived from G. Alan Marlatt's famous urge surfing approach to working with addiction and relapse prevention, we can also apply this surfing of the experience with emotions.

PRACTICE POINT: Surfing the Emotion Wave

When an emotion is triggered through an initiating event, choose to 'sit' with the wave of the emotion as it moves through the different stages.

Be alert and aware to all aspects of the emotional wave: body sensations, thoughts, urges to take action.

Allow the whole experience to be there as much as possible, neither feeding nor avoiding the process. Note judgements and beliefs; note the rise in intensity and the lessening of intensity when that occurs.

It can take practice to understand that it is okay to sit in a high energy state without acting on impulses or dissipating the intensity. Instead, observe.

IN SUMMARY

This chapter focuses on the 'gap' between something happening that triggers an emotion and the point at which the emotion is clearly identified. Identifying and increasing awareness of parts of the emotion process allow for a sense of deeper understanding, control and management. This, in turn, enhances the capacity for choice around expression or containment, for verbally communicating what has occurred emotionally, and viewing things from a realistic perspective.

TAKEAWAY PRACTICES

- Practise mindfulness/awareness of the process of emotion, noticing the different moving parts.

- **Map Out** the emotion process through reflecting on an emotion experience as a whole. Write it out either in hindsight, or during the emotion when possible.

- Bring awareness to experiencing secondary emotions and practise identifying the primary or core emotion as well as the secondary emotion.

- Learn to clearly identify and name the emotion, using the list of emotions in Chapter 1 to broaden your emotion vocabulary.

- Practise awareness around expression or containment of emotions when an emotion arises and experiment with the ideas presented to support each.

- Practise **Surfing the Emotion Wave**.

CHAPTER 4

Luck of the Draw

As humans we are born into a world where external shaping forces impact the way in which we experience emotions, as well as influence our relationship with our emotional selves. And this shaping occurs from day one of life. These forces operate on multiple levels—social, cultural, and personal—varying for each of us due to our different circumstances, uniquely drawn together. The environment we grow up in also shapes us according to the conditions and demands it places on us and our family or caregivers.

What do we mean by these external shaping forces?

As a child, I often visited friends at home after school. The differences between how my own family operated and how a friend's family operated, were frequently very tangible and surprising. As children, we are born sensitive and I recall immediately picking up on different behaviour and attitudes shown within other families: between the adults, the adults and the children, and between siblings.

For example, there could be different boundaries set around what was okay for us to do, around the way food was dealt with and around going to school. There were rules about what you could touch and not touch, where you could be and what you could do while playing. There were differences too, in how involved and present the adults were in what we kids were doing. Every now and then there would even be the novelty of a mum or dad who wanted to play too.

Without realising, I was tapping into the different culture that develops within groups of people. Family units are a prime example of a social group where radical shaping and influencing occurs on each of us. As a child, going to another family home was sometimes akin to going a different country. Some cultures were much closer to my own, with many familiar, recognisable aspects. Other times I felt like a foreigner, somewhat in awe of the strangeness that I experienced, sometimes uncomfortable. It was a prime example of the first broadening of my mind to the bigger, wider world.

Every family develops its own unique culture despite similarities and shared common ground.

KEY CONCEPT: Culture and Shaping

The word *culture* describes a collective agreement on what is considered 'normal' in a group of people. Normal is what becomes viewed as desirable—expected, acceptable behaviour and beliefs for functioning in life. Commonality facilitates belonging within a group of people and belonging to the group harks back to the issue of survival. Being part of the group—belonging, being accepted, fitting in—all relate to the fight-or-flight system, if membership to the group feels at risk. Subscribing to the culture of the group therefore matters in terms of fitting in.

Culture exerts an enormous influence on us as we develop: it conditions us; it shapes our behaviour and thinking and asserts certain esteemed values on us to live by. This is what is meant by 'shaping'. Just as the wind and water of the storm can carve and mould the shoreline through the forces they exert, so too do the forces of the people we grow up around, the community we belong to and other factors that constitute the world we inhabit. Over the years, these consistent forces exert quite a shaping impact.

NATURE *AND* NURTURE

A quick note: this chapter focuses on how people come to be who they are, what shapes them and effects them as they mature and develop emotionally. It taps into the old 'nature versus nurture' question present in science since the early 19th century, which has asked the question: how much of who we are is to do with our genetic programming, hardwired into the genes we carry, or the shaping, influencing environment we are nurtured within as we grow and develop?

Most recently the nature versus nurture debate has evolved into the nature *and* nurture debate, acknowledging that both play their part.

This interplay of nurturing factors with the genetic potential we carry, reframes this whole debate, and is the focus of this key area and how it impacts on our emotional reality.

EMOTIONAL INHERITANCE

For all the differences in culture and our version of 'normal'— where we belong and what that looks like—the common ground for us is that we are all born into a context, an environment. And amongst the many things that this environment provides us with, are messages and demands on how we feel, how we should aim to feel, and how we feel about feeling.

The truth is that there is no universal 'normal' and that is good news. Particularly in Western, democratic societies we are free to choose as long as we do no harm to others. But there is an inheritance of sorts that profoundly affects who we end up becoming. Emotional content, shaping and influence comes as part of the package deal into which we are born.

We receive messages about:
- how to view emotions generally
- how specific types of emotions are regarded
- how to deal with emotions when they occur
- how others regard our emotions.

These communications require a response and we do respond to the demands placed upon us one way or another.

Broadly, there are three basic ways we may respond or react to the messages we receive:
- We accept the messages. We take them onboard and go along with what we are asked to do. We comply with them.
- We reject them. We rebel against what we are asked to do. We object.
- We struggle with them and struggle to resolve how we go with them. We do not agree but struggle to differ. We try to comply but cannot pull it off.

Often, we try to first comply then branch out into other options if unable to sustain the compliance. The response or reaction we choose then flows on throughout our lifetime unless we update these messages consciously, either affirming them as something that we like and that fits for us, or replacing them if they do not fit and work for us in our lives.

LUCK OF THE DRAW

On a fundamental level, it can be seen to be the 'luck of the draw' on where we end up, who we end up with as our family and community, who we are raised by, into what cultural, economic and societal conditions we are born. Some, through their religious faith and belief systems might disagree about the 'luck of the draw' way in which we end up where we do, and I certainly do not aim to challenge that.

However, the point I make is that as a babe we are born into something not of our making; that we then receive, absorb, and need to negotiate with for the rest of our lives. There are facts beyond our control.

KEY CONCEPT: Environment and Person-in-Environment

As a social worker, one of the essential models for practice, which differentiates the social work profession from many other health professions, is recognition of the need to see the individual person holistically. It is termed **'person-in-environment'**. Another related theory, the Ecological Theory, highlights the interconnectedness of people to their environment, that each of us is part of a broader ecosystem that strikes a certain balance amongst all the parts that exist within it.

The central idea is that a person is always intimately linked in with their circumstances and cannot be taken out of their environment and set of circumstances if we want to truly see and understand that person for who they are (and become).

Factors that are significant within the person-in-environment include: gender, family and social networks, health, faith or religion, ethnicity, and economic security.

REFLECTION POINT

Identifying your personal environmental factors

Reflect on and write a list of the factors of your environment as a child, guided by each the following explorations.

> **gender** (and any shifts in gender)
> How did you feel you represented your gender? Were there any concerns or issues from within yourself or others?
>
> Did this generate any particular emotions for you?

➤ **family network**
Did you have a continued family arrangement, or did it change? Did it feel secure? Was it dominated by any issues or family members?

Did this generate any particular emotions for you?

➤ **social connections**
What was the social situation for yourself and your family? Were you part of any particular society or community? Was there a wider community present?

Did this generate any particular emotions for you?

➤ **health or disability factors**
With you or others in your family were there any prevailing health concerns, including diseases or illnesses, mental health conditions, addictions, intellectual or physical impairments?

Did this generate any particular emotions for you?

➤ **ethnic background**
Did your family identify with any particular ethnicity? Were you a minority or majority in the wider community that you lived in? What are the qualities or characteristics of that ethnic group for you?

Did this generate any particular emotions for you?

➤ **faith or religion**
Growing up were you and/or your family part of a spiritual practice: a faith or religion?

Did this generate any particular emotions for you?

➤ **socio-economic status**
Were you aware of the level of financial security growing up? How was money for your family and the resources money can buy? How did this impact your life?

Did this generate any particular emotions for you?

As you identify your person-in-environment facts notice if there are any other factors not covered in the categories and add those in to complete your unique picture.

BENEFITS OF UNDERSTANDING EXTERNAL FORCES

So, what are the benefits in identifying the external messages around emotions that you have received? And the contribution of environmental factors?

Let's have a closer look.

Increased self-understanding

By bringing attention and focus to how external influences have shaped your emotional experience in life, self-understanding naturally increases. This self-understanding increases clarity around emotional experiences, reducing confusion. By understanding ourselves better through the demands that have been imposed upon us and our responses, we gain insight into what has shaped us emotionally.

Provides a more accurate sense of self

Seeing these influences clearly, allows a fresh and more accurate perspective on yourself—what is actually you as a person, versus what has been imposed on you from the outside. Our identity is not always innately derived, springing up from within, even if that is how we have come to view it.

The hard, cold reality is that we all take on ideas, beliefs, and values from those around us, and are often directly instructed to do so. We can be told who we are and what we are like as a person, including our emotional selves with emotional consequences.

As children, adults often project their own hopes and dreams upon us with good intentions, or to simply control the outcome, believing their way is the right way. Separating what is yours truly and what you *choose* to imbibe, versus what belongs to other people, can be extremely liberating, increasing a more confident and conscious identity of who you are as a person.

Validates the impacts of life experiences and circumstances

Our history matters in ways that we often cannot see, precisely because it has become our version of 'normal'—the only 'normal' we know. By fleshing out the facts of messages received about emotions, teasing out how you observed the people around you deal with their own emotions, that in turn modelled the way you should do it, can be very validating.

It often confirms our true perceptions on what we were experiencing but might not have had validated.

Increasing choices moving forward

Once we see the outside influences more clearly (and this is a process that can take time and continue throughout life) our capacity to consciously choose what we do around our emotional life significantly increases. Unhealthy, unhelpful ideas and attitudes, attitudes that do not reflect our values and who we aspire to be as a person, coping mechanisms and approaches to dealing with and managing emotions that do not work well, can be replaced with more aligned, effective options.

Or, with choice, we can simply experiment with other ways of responding to our feelings, and over time, refine what we stand for and what works for us. If in doubt, try something new, do something different, borrow ideas from what we observe others doing, and create a new path forward.

DISCERNING THE HELPFUL FROM THE UNHELPFUL

It is important to note that some messages we receive *are* healthy, desirable, and serve us well in life. They fit for us and our values as a person; they support us in living our life and functioning emotionally. They are not something that we need nor want to question and change. This is usually because they contain a respectful, healthy and effective approach towards emotions.

It is also because what you have received from the outside, has fitted and worked for you, and therefore, you have made it your own. It is no longer externally imposed and foreign.

Unhelpful ideas and secondary emotional reactions

Unhelpful attitudes tend to be ones that are invalidating, dismissive and judgemental of our emotions and feelings. They often disrupt and subvert the actual process of experiencing an emotion (as outlined in the previous chapter). Due to the disruption to the emotion process these kinds of ideas contribute to emotional struggles and stormy weather by complicating and subverting emotional reality.

Unhelpful attitudes and ideas are a main cause of secondary emotions being generated—the secondary emotional reaction to the original or core emotion.

Examples of this are:
- When I feel envious and jealous, I am a bad person because they are 'bad' emotions, so when I feel these things, I then feel guilty and ashamed
- When I feel happy and proud of myself, I then become scared because I was told not to get too full of myself
- When I feel upset and about to cry, I then feel embarrassed, as I was always told that crying is a sign of weakness
- When I feel love, I become scared of rejection as I was told that other people cannot be trusted.

Unfitting ideas and attitudes create inner conflict if they go against our own innate, actual experience.

DEVELOPING A CRITICAL GAZE

The amazing thing is that while emotions are like the superhighway of our lives—the palpable stuff that influences and motivates us, the signposts of what matters to us and whether something is going well or not—emotions are usually never openly, pragmatically addressed, as we develop. Yet we need to learn about managing them. Roughly put, growing up is about taming our emotions to a great extent —the civilising of our raw, primal, emotionally immediate young selves and ideally developing a maturity in handling them in ourselves and others.

So, how do we learn about having emotions?

If you are like me and the many people I have encountered personally and professionally, there will be a variety of answers to that question. None are usually consistent or coherent; very few include any formal education system, or direct focus on emotions unto themselves.

Most people learn about emotions through indirect, haphazard means. This includes a lot of watching what others do, receiving indirect communications about our emotions and emotional selves. It includes sensing attitudes acted out in social situations such as with family, at school, places of worship and other community groups, that may never be openly stated or spoken. We must 'pick it up' as we go. And often the very people we learn from may not be comfortable, skilled or mature in their own emotional lives.

The messages we receive about emotions also frequently tend to be underlined by a broad negative attitude. Over many centuries and within most cultures, spiritual traditions and philosophies, emotions have been viewed as a risk and danger to maintaining order within society and amongst people. Emotions have been pegged as the aspect of human nature that is a sign of being out-of-control and irrational in nature. Many societal messages have condemned too much emotion as akin to being weak and a sign of being 'crazy'. Across many cultures it has been aligned with the feminine and the flaws attributed to femininity in patriarchal-based societies and religions.

In beginning to do the work suggested in this chapter, and more broadly in this book, we need to develop a healthy ability to be critical of what has been served up to us as 'normal' around our emotions. There is a need to take a step back and seek a fresh view, not accept these ideas and attitudes as the only truth, to be critical of things, but in an intelligent, thoughtful and constructive way. The reflection points in this book are designed to help cultivate questioning, to break some of the automatic programs that we run without question, to develop a healthy 'critical gaze'.

REFLECTION POINT

Take a moment and have a think about how you learnt to understand, navigate, and appreciate your emotions.

How did you learn to live your emotional self?

Was there a direct communication or guidance around emotions?

Did it occur during your education at school, did it happen through a parental figure, did it occur through another key person?

DIRECT AND INDIRECT COMMUNICATION

Messages can be given directly and spoken. For example, children can be told that they need to stop crying, that they are rude when they feel angry, that they are too excitable. Adults can be told that their emotion is not appropriate at work or in other situations, that they are overreacting to something. Both adults and children can be given the message of being 'too emotional' very directly with words.

Often, however, the messages we receive are not delivered in words. They are not verbalised but are still received loud and clear. Interestingly, it is the communication of emotions that can tend to happen through nonverbal communication. We get the message though the behaviour and responses of the people that matter to us: unspoken, subtle cues expressed through the body. See the table below for a comparison of communication pathways.

Direct Communication	Nonverbal, indirect communication
Words are spoken to convey message	Tone of voice
	Body posture (slouching versus upright)
	Facial expression
	Hand expression
	Colour of skin
	Touch
	Breathing rate and depth
	Gestures
	Movement
	Eye contact and expression

MIXED MESSAGES

Mixed messages are also extremely common around emotions. They are when one thing is said but through the nonverbal cues of behaviour and emotion felt in the other person, a different, often conflicting message is received.

Here are a few classic examples and with them I want you to tune into the conflicting emotional impact for the person receiving this message:

- A client was told that no matter what her father would always love her and support her, but she got a clear feeling of disapproval around wanting to pursue a career as an artist from him.

- A child was told that her mother would always be there for her but when she approached her, the mother constantly reacted with seeming anger and impatience.
- A manager told a worker that they had a positive response to disability in the workplace, but when she disclosed her depression, was met with a lack of empathy and constructive flexibility.

THREE LEVELS OF SHAPING AND INFLUENCING EMOTIONS

Broadly speaking, there are three useful levels to look at when considering some of the types of messages received around your emotions.

These are:
- broad, social, cultural, larger collective messages
- personal, intimate collective (family and personal circles) messages
- gender-based messages.

Let's take a closer look at these.

SOCIAL MESSAGES AROUND EMOTIONS

Broad social messages around emotions are literally broadcast to us en masse all our waking hours. They are delivered to us through popular media in a potent way; through television, radio, social media, drama and movies, magazines, billboard advertising and other consumable media we are all exposed to. These messages are also delivered to us through being in school, a workplace, and in other groups of people.

Historically, messages about emotions have long tentacles back in time. Emotions have often been viewed as at odds with the rational and logical. Broad social messages about emotions are dominating ideas that can be based on the dominant religion or codes of values and behaviour within a society. Certain emotions are given support and esteem, are set up as the stuff to aim for, while other emotions are regarded in a negative way.

PERSONAL HISTORY MESSAGES ON EMOTION

Examining our family messages about emotions can be challenging because they are often given in an indirect way, almost floating in the air we breathe. There is a saying that it 'is difficult to see the wood for the trees' and this is true for all communications around emotions; we tend to just live with our version of 'normal' as it is received. We are so close to it that we do not have any observing distance, taking a step back to get a clear view of something and be critical of it.

REFLECTION POINT

Were there any predominant emotions in your house growing up?

Were there any emotions that were not allowed and were frowned upon?

Were you told any direct messages about feelings?

What would happen if you were upset?

What kind of reaction did you receive from the various people around you?

Did you have a sense of safety with your emotions?

Was there anyone you felt safest around emotionally growing up?

Were there mixed messages, or conflicting messages?

GENDER-BASED MESSAGES ON EMOTIONS

Across most cultures there is a difference in expectations placed on the different genders and this includes with emotions.

Gender-based messages tap into both the collective, broad messages about emotions and play out in the personal, family level. As a child I certainly received a message that is commonplace for females of all ages: it was not feminine to be angry; women are not allowed to be angry. I noted that when I felt angry or frustrated that I would cry instead. To feel angry was to feel wrong and it was scary to try to manage it when it came up, as I felt I should not have anger.

Equally, I recall males were not meant to cry. Crying was viewed as feminine and a sign of emotional weakness. For a boy to cry was for him to look 'soft' and sensitive versus the ideal of the masculine being characterised by strength and toughness.

REFLECTION POINT

Recall the messages about your gender as you grew up. What feelings was this linked to and how do you recall responding to these messages about what was acceptable and desirable?

KEY CONCEPT: Internal and External

A helpful distinction to be aware of is to note the internal versus external parts of your experience.

Internal refers to the inner workings of you as a person that no-one else is privy to. These include our thoughts, feelings, beliefs, sensations and states. It includes our self-talk (what we say to ourselves in a running commentary as we move through our days) and the judgements we make on all that we encounter.

External refers to what we are aware of beyond our skin. This includes the people in our lives as well as the external environment that others can be in direct contact with as well.

Often there is an exchange between these two as shown in the following diagram. This chapter is concerned about the exchange that can occur with strong external messages from significant others as well as environmental factors. We can internalise things from the outside as well as project things to the outside, externalising inner aspects of our experience.

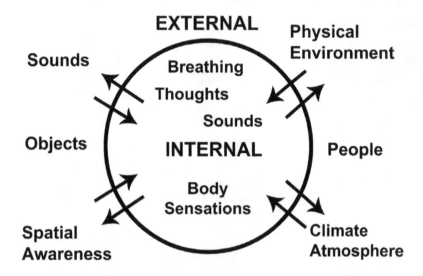

Internal and External Factors

In the spirit of utilising awareness as a main tool, the power of presence to emotions is to notice where certain ideas and beliefs actually come from.

I cannot tell you over the years how many people, after describing highly critical parents in their childhood—parents for who no academic excellence was ever quite enough and left the person driven to keep forever striving—will actually then say to me, 'But you know they are right'. These people will then recite a list of evidence of their need to improve. The message of their childhood and feelings about themselves is well and truly internalised and now they don't need their parents to be there anymore; they do it to themselves.

PRACTICE POINT: Mindfulness of Internal and External

Sit in a comfortable position.

Close your eyes and become aware of your internal reality in this moment.

Note anything present including breathing, body sensations and movements, any thoughts or activity of the mind (images, commentary, judgements, ideas), as well as any emotions that may be present.

Take a few minutes to note your internal reality without censoring, engaging with or seeking to change what you observe.

Now shift your awareness to the environment beyond your skin. Notice any sounds, weather, temperature, presence of other people or other elements outside of you. Gently open your eyes and take in the visual reality you are placed in.

Take a few minutes to note your external reality without censoring, engaging with or seeking to change what you observe. Observe.

Take a moment to shift your attention mindfully between the internal versus the external facets of your perception.

This practice helps develop a clearer capacity to note internal and external factors that impact you as they occur, to tune into reality of the moment and distinguish between within and without.

IN SUMMARY

Society, culture and factors in our personal life all shape us emotionally, including gender. Such influences are driven by common social norms, and spiritual ideals and behaviour established and pre-existing in the family or group we are born into. If these messages are not healthy, they can contribute to difficulties, compounding emotions and struggle within, when emotions naturally arise. Equally, environmental factors can influence our emotional set-up.

Identifying the messages received clearly, helps build self-understanding, awareness and the capacity to choose more updated stances on what is okay and what is effective in being with your emotions. Developing the ability to critically question in a constructive way, assists in being clear about external messaging received.

TAKEAWAY PRACTICES

- Reflect on the impacts of your environment at different times in your life, including the following aspects:

    - ➢ gender (and any shifts in gender)

    - ➢ family network

    - ➢ social connections

    - ➢ health or disability factors

    - ➢ ethnic background

    - ➢ faith or religion

    - ➢ socio-economic status.

- Practise noticing verbal versus nonverbal communication in yourself and others when in social situations.

- Practise noticing mixed messages from other people in your life and how you pick this up on an emotional level.

- Reflect on the messages around your emotions that you received on the three levels:

    - ➢ social and cultural

    - ➢ personal or family

    - ➢ gender based.

- Practise **Mindfulness of the Internal and External** in different environments.

CHAPTER 5

Safe Harbour
in the Storm

When an emotion or multiple emotions are triggered, and we are in the midst of feeling, the 'process' of feeling is in motion. In other words, the train has left the station—and as we've discussed in previous chapters, many things occur inside us.

The fullness of action can lead to a sense of confusion or disorganisation within during this process—of changeability and flux, of rapid firing of associated emotion-based thoughts and memories, of physiological changes—all of which can create a kind of emotional storm effect. With emotions moving, it can feel intense; it can feel scary or distressing; it can create confusion and a sense of being overwhelmed or swamped; or it can be just downright irritating. A strong desire may arise to want to get rid of all this 'goddamned' feeling. This is a common type of secondary reaction to the original feeling that can contribute to a sense of struggle and complexity (as covered in Chapter 3).

With the activation of the fight-or-flight system, the ability to rationalise and think in a helpful way becomes affected. When the survival system is activated, energy is diverted away from the normal bodily functions to areas that help us react to danger, including impairing of the higher order, logical and rational thinking capacity of the brain. The more primitive parts of the brain are busy signalling via the nervous system (with electrical messages) and via the hormonal system (with chemical messages), responses to incite as well as alternatively dampen certain bodily functions as part of the emergency response. Moreover, the thinking or cognition that prevails can become dominated by the emotional forces and participate in the project of seeking to identify and head-off perceived dangers.

KEY CONCEPT: The Negativity Bias

The mind has the tendency to head-off into 'worst case scenario' territory, predicting or anticipating—with trepidation—awful, challenging, and difficult results from the current situation. This is frequently married with tapping into any past experiences that seem similar and relevant to what is happening now. In psychology, this is called the **negativity bias**.

This bias describes a hardwired cognitive tendency to focusing in on potential risk and danger playing out. It is deeply connected to the fight-or-flight system, and to survival.

I recently experienced a blindsiding, rapid-firing emotional storm. It was 'live action' for writing this book, literally, and my negative bias took full flight.

I live in a building that is twenty storeys high and has two elevators to access the building. Every now and again an elevator will stop working and usually gets fixed within the day.

But recently, something different happened.

One of the elevators stopped and was out of order over the weekend, with a sign announcing that it would be fixed on Monday. Monday came and went, and we remained with one elevator. At peak times it was full, with long waits to get in. A few people graffitied the sign: 'Fixed on Monday' was added to with, 'this year?' next to it. Someone then added the following year in reply.

My own thought processes began to become tainted by the alarm and stress arising in me as this situation went on and on for days. This thinking included:

'Surely, in this day and age, an elevator outage shouldn't take this long to fix?'

'This is highly unusual. Something must be really wrong.'

My thoughts turned to the company servicing our lift:

'They must not be trying.'

'We are not getting the right service.'

'This is being mishandled … the lift maintenance company can't seem to handle this breakdown.'

'This is going to be very expensive.'

'We are being tricked out of our warranty by big multinationals who maximise their profits and have unfair legal clauses in contracts to protect themselves …'

I think that you get the picture of where this was going in my thinking!

In my mind and feelings, the situation began to look as if the worst was occurring. I felt in danger and was fearful, with anxiety and anger growing within me. I wanted a solution and quickly. My mind went to the scenario of what would happen if the other lift broke down and people on higher floors couldn't get to their apartments. I imagined people blaming the building management, and suing the building, that the building would have to pay for people's accommodation and for the inconvenience of the whole situation.

As I began to recognise my spiralling emotional state, I identified factors that were fuelling my emotional stress. These included:

- The building manager did not have all the information about where it was all up to and could only tell me so much. However, even with details remaining unclear it did not actually mean that more was not happening behind the scenes (as humans we like security, remember)

- Previously I had lived in another building where one resident was very litigious and regularly threatening legal action over matters that were beyond our control (hence why I moved!)
- I was stressed about what others were thinking and who they might blame (a personal vulnerability and pattern from my own personal history)
- I was worried about the cost involved if it was something catastrophic (striking at basic fight-or-flight survival through economic security).

Looking objectively at the situation I identified the facts of the situation in the same way a police officer or court of law identifies hard and fast, factually-based evidence. The facts were:
- the first lift had broken down and was in process of being fixed
- the lift maintenance company had been visiting the building numerous times
- the second lift did break down but when I rang the building manager, he already knew about it and had called the maintenance company. The second lift was restored to working order within about twenty minutes.

All the above were the facts; that was what *actually* happened. Simple. Straightforward. Taken care of.

If I had been able to stay in the present moment, with reality as it presented itself, without subscribing to emotional, inner embellishment, then my emotional reaction might still have been there but would have been very different in intensity and dynamics. It would have felt significantly smaller in nature and the feelings would not have spiralled and compounded as they did by worries and past experiences.

Reality has a certain quality about it, versus anticipation and fear projections.

THE PRESENT MOMENT AS A RESOURCE

Staying in the present moment is vital and important to successfully handling emotional challenges. It allows us to better understand what we are dealing with, navigate it, and glean the good stuff to be had from the experience. By being with what actually *is*, versus what escalates in the mind as possible (the negativity bias ramping up unconsciously) we can respond rather than react.

KEY CONCEPT: Response and Reaction

In psychology and personal growth fields, a distinction between a *reaction* and a *response* is an essential and helpful staple for self-questioning. Related to circumstances where our emotions arise and play a central role in the lived experience, this concept highlights a difference in the type of action we may end up taking.

A **reaction** is instant—a fast and rapid action that is fuelled by quick assessment, with a narrow, immediate view of things. It comes from the unconscious of our minds and may be fuelled by our own beliefs and past experiences. Often these reactions can keep firing, leading to a cascade of reactions. Considered thinking about the consequences of the reaction, of the future, taking a longer-term view, tend to all be lost during a moment of reacting. Reactions *can* work out okay and achieve a desired outcome, however, more often people regret their reactions if the initial assessment of the circumstances was not accurate. Reactions are fast, impulse-driven, and usually narrow in vision. They can compound challenges in life if not appropriate to the circumstances.

A **response** comes more slowly—it can include input from both the conscious and unconscious parts of our mind but tends to be more considered and alert to ongoing consequences, and the bigger picture. Actions that flow out of a response tend to be aligned more fully with your own values, taking both yourself and others into the equation, as well as the facts, feelings, perceptions and assessment of the situation.

KEY CONCEPT: Low and High Roads of Brain Processing

Responding versus reacting can be further explained through an understanding of the distinctly different neurological pathways of each action. Psychologist and neuroscientist Joseph LeDoux conducted research that explored these pathways of fear and other emotional responses which he describes as the **'low' and 'high' roads**.

The concept concerns how a human brain processes stimulus received from our environment and influences us to either react or respond according to how the information is processed.

The low road represents the earliest part of the brain in action, where the core processing of the fight-or-flight response to perceived threats takes place. It is a quick and instinctive reaction to an immediate need.

The high road represents information being directed to the newer, higher order brain processes where our capacity to assess is slower and more sophisticated. It takes longer but is a fuller, more complex response.

THE POWER OF THE PRESENT MOMENT FOR EMOTIONS

This chapter focuses on staying in the moment as an effective strategy for avoiding the worst of an emotional storm's wild, whipping winds and perils. It represents a practice that aims to shift reaction to the possibility of responding instead. By utilising mindfulness skills, being in the present moment with what actually is, in the here and now of our existence, we assist ourselves in a multitude of ways.

BENEFITS OF STAYING IN THE PRESENT MOMENT

A simpler perspective

By taking refuge in the simplicity of now, life is infinitely easier to deal with. Orienting yourself to the here and now present moment creates a safe harbour from the storm that might be brewing or in full flight. Reality can be most fully encountered when we bring our focus and attention into this moment as totally as we are able. This is when we seek to deal with what is real, literally standing before us; from here available options can be identified and explored in an authentic way.

Fears, dreads or anticipated outcomes can certainly lie in our thoughts and feelings as part of this present moment. However, we see them much more clearly as part of our thinking and feeling processes, part of an activation of the fight-or-flight system, versus being part of the present truth and truly representative of what is occurring. This is a fundamental difference. Observing our feelings and thought processes in a mindful way, in the moment, significantly shifts the perspective that we hold them in.

Seeing more clearly

When we are hijacked by our emotions and our fight-or-flight system is activated, it feels like the dangerous things are already happening and are part and parcel of reality. This often tends not to be true. Moreover, this tends to be characteristic of operating in survival mode, where the view of reality is distorted to see indicators of what you are fearful of and threatened by.

Anchoring in the present moment—the safe harbour in the storm—helps to see the situation more clearly and undercut distorting reactions within. Being present enables you to identify inner reactions for what they are and see the external factors more clearly and separate to inner factors.

Tolerating not knowing if that is the fact

The desire to jump into a full assessment of triggering circumstances and into future outcomes is often fuelled by the discomfort of not knowing yet the outcome or resolution to a situation. If you stay with reality, it often includes not yet knowing. As previously stated, we are hardwired to not like that, to resist insecurity, and head towards seeming security and clarity with a vengeance.

Being present in the now assists us with tolerating the insecurity of what could happen if things are unclear; to not subscribing yet to the projected, unsubstantiated fears in order to relieve the state of not knowing.

To say to yourself, 'I don't know the answer yet' can be both relieving and validating of the truth of the moment and the feelings that come with that.

Identifying the past polluting the present view

Being in the present moment helps us avoid falling into the past. It allows past outcomes to be related to the current situation in our mind's eye, but not be carried into the current emotional state, lock, stock, and barrel. Having past experiences triggered can add to the emotionality experienced, colouring reality. Becoming enmeshed in the past can distort accurately assessing what is happening now.

Yes, certain past experiences can be relevant, where similarities exist or the same person is involved and history can contribute to current assessment. However, it is how this past is handled that makes the difference. Being mindful and present to all the stimuli you note in the current moment, assists in recognising the past for what it is: the past. From this clearer stance anything of similarity can be more accurately assessed and more effectively used if relevant.

The power of being present to emotions

Practising staying in the present moment, with what is, holds no risk. Not only does it assist with not adding unnecessarily to current challenges emotionally, it also increases the capacity to be with any emotions present in a significant way.

There is a need to feel the feelings, to sit with them and give them space to be, that has a transforming effect. It validates the feeling, it melts resistance or added embellishments, and facilitates acknowledgment, acceptance and often a certain kind of peace or reckoning with what may have triggered the emotion. In being present simply to the emotion and feeling, much is gained.

Accessing your supports when you need them

In staying present, available securities, resources and positive factors are not missed, as can occur when in survival mode and holding a distorted view of the situation. Being mindfully present helps broaden the view of the moment from the narrow lens of survival and emotionality, allowing a more accurate view of things as they are, and resources and supports that are available.

The risks of not being present

If we do not harness the present as a resource for managing intense emotions, we risk:

- Being influenced by a whole range of things that may not be based in the current reality we are seeking to handle. Emotions can be amplified by a whole cascade of negative thinking (the negativity bias) and memories or old feelings from past events getting triggered by association.
- Being hijacked by the emotion process in an unhelpful way, with no observing distance to it, and no genuine grounds to respond to challenges in an effective way, here and now.
- Missing the opportunity to be present to the emotions in a validating and enrichening way.

CULTIVATING AWARENESS OF THE PRESENT MOMENT

This key is a recap of practising mindfulness—orienting oneself and one's awareness to this very moment, right now. Through cultivating being in the moment, the moment becomes a primary refuge—a safe harbour during emotional storms.

To bring yourself and your awareness into the present moment is a practice. No matter how much you utilise this skill, it is always a practice. Some days will be easier than others, depending on what you might be facing, the level of emotion and stress present and how much you have going on that challenges maintaining your attention to current reality. Fortunately, there is no right or wrong, no 'made it or didn't make it', or goal that you are striving for beyond practising being present.

PRACTICES FOR TUNING INTO THE MOMENT

PRACTICE POINT: 5-4-3-2-1 Senses Counting

This brief exercise is excellent for bringing a person back into their current environment, a critical aspect of being present in the now. This exercise is especially relevant when there is a lot of movement and action within you—emotions, thoughts and sensations—that may be overwhelming and distracting. It is a simple practice to reach for when you are literally feeling in the middle of and at the mercy of an emotional storm. It utilises the five senses of our physical body, which are always available in present moment awareness.

The process goes like this:
- Begin by noting five things you can see in your present environment. Look around and state to yourself five things you can see.
- Next, note four things you can hear. Take time to listen and again state to yourself four different things you can hear that are part of the present moment. Some sounds may be close and obvious, some more distant, and some may even be within your own body.
- Next, note to yourself three things you can feel, tuning into the sense of touch. Again, state each of these to yourself as you count them off.
- Next, see if you can note two things in the present moment you can smell. This can be subtle and more challenging but see what is present and take a moment to seek out two smells.
- Lastly, note one taste that might be present to you right now. Take this moment to tune into your mouth and the tastes that might be there.

PRACTICE POINT: Box Breathing

This simple practice assists in times of high emotion by bringing focus to the current moment, with both the breath and counting as anchors. This practice gives your mind a task to do, helps to settle into the present despite the emotions that may be active within.

Find a speed that feels relaxed and comfortable to do this practice. It might take a few goes of trying the cycle I am describing, to work out how you manage the pace of doing this.

The steps are:
- Tune into the inhalation or in breath, counting to four as we breathe in silently: 1-2-3-4.
- When you have reached the end of your inhalation, pause and hold the inhalation for four: 1-2-3-4 counting silently within.
- Allow the exhalation to start and count to four silently as you breathe out: 1-2-3-4.
- When you reach the end of the exhalation, again pause and hold the breath out for four: counting 1-2-3-4 silently.
- Repeat this cycle for the desired practice time.

Take a moment and try this now in the pattern described and represented in the diagram. See if you can settle in and do a few cycles. Take note of how this affects you.

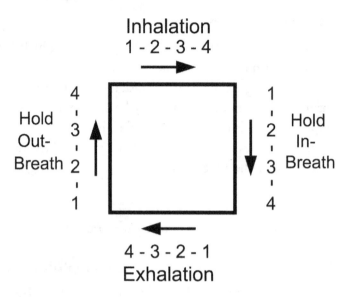

Box Breathing Cycle

Tip: Ensure that you feel comfortable with managing your breathing, and if needed, take a moment to stop and take a few slow steady breaths. Then try again, until you master the pace that fits for you where the issue of getting enough air (and *not* triggering your fight-or-flight system by raising concerns around getting enough air) does not arise.

With regular practise of these mindfulness exercises, and being present to this current moment, what *is* can emerge and be seen more closely. It aids in recognising elements at play, and patterns of behaviour and thinking, in both yourself and others. It aids in clearly recognising the external circumstances too.

I spent many years living in India, a country that certainly contrasted to first world living with all the in-built safety and legislated order that I was used to. From time to time I needed to leave the country, travelling back to Australia or elsewhere for a break. This required road travel over several hours to the capital of Mumbai (known for many years by the anglicised name of Bombay).

Throughout my life I had always been a relaxed traveller, feeling excitement and a sense of freedom and adventure that I thrive on to this day. India certainly dealt that up in abundance and in my initial travels I had mainly explored via local buses of the cheapest class—open windows, dust and all kinds of weather rushing through, sparse interiors, frequently overcrowded, and with a very different approach to driving than I was used to. The bus often veered onto the wrong side of the road, intimidating other drivers into giving way in a head-on situation. It was fast, furious and seemingly chaotic. Often, with near misses during head-on 'drive-downs', when the driver of the bus managed to triumph, the rest of the passengers would loudly cheer, seemingly immune to any sense of the danger we had all been in just moments before.

Having been used to travelling in these kinds of conditions for many years, I was taken by surprise one day when I suddenly started to get very apprehensive and fearful about travelling. It was as if I had suddenly become highly tuned to all the risks of this chaotic country on the road.

On one particular trip to Mumbai, my fear came to a peak and I felt incredibly apprehensive about being in an accident, extremely pessimistic and anxious in my thinking and emotions. During the trip, which was in the middle of the night (just to add to the challenging conditions), I was extremely tense, and every shudder of the bus felt increasingly terrifying. At this time of the night the highway was dominated by big trucks and buses like mine, all hurtling emphatically towards their destination. My mind was going a hundred miles an hour, working over and over on the dilemma I was in. I was exhausted and my fear peaked to a point where it became unbearable.

At this moment, my focus seemed to shift, perhaps through exhausting myself and hitting a limit. I recognised how much I was fully resisting and fighting the situation I was in. This meant physically that my body was very tense, as I braced and resisted every single shudder and bump on the road. No wonder I was exhausted. Indian roads are full of bumps and holes and I felt every one with heightened vigilance and significant inner reaction.

In that moment, I came to view my situation more openly, mindfully and one could say, realistically. I saw that I was swept up in my own emotional story, and it was compounding my suffering. I was resisting reality and it subsequently left me extremely stressed and exhausted.

I consciously relaxed my body and allowed the infinite shudders and swerves of the bus to sway me. I recognised that I clearly did not have control over much in my current situation. Tensing and resisting every movement of the bus achieved nothing in changing the situation; I was in the hands of the driver and that was that.

In that moment I surrendered to the motion. I brought my focus to my physical body and allowed it to move with the bus. I accepted that I was in the hands of the driver, and one who no doubt had driven this road in these conditions all his life. I also noted a sense of relief and freedom in this surrender. I came into the moment and was able to let go of the previous storm of thought and emotion.

Engaging with the body in the moment gave me a new anchor, that shifted my whole perspective and experience. In fact, the rocking motion of my body, as I sat in my seat, became somewhat soothing and supported the newborn acceptance with what was.

This experience represents the power of this key—the safe harbour of the storm is through being present to what is in its entirety. Mindfulness offers shelter and a refuge from being battered and swept up in the power of the storm. It is not avoidance or removal from the reality, but rather embedding oneself in current reality, in a way that is both protective and wise. It facilitates a shift in our relationship to circumstances within and without.

IN SUMMARY

The truth is that all we have is this moment and therefore all we need to be with, attend to and take care of, is the 'now' of our lives. Being present provides the greatest potential for responding effectively to what is. It offers a safe harbour during emotional storms, where fight-or-flight thinking and the added fuelling of emotions with past experiences and apprehension around the future, can be graciously sidestepped. Practising bringing yourself into the present moment helps increase contact with reality and undercuts embellished emotional distress by future-focused fears and worries.

TAKEAWAY PRACTICES

- During your day notice any moments where you may react versus respond to a situation. Notice the difference in taking the low or high roads of reaction and response.

- Practise **5-4-3-2-1 Senses Counting** in various environments, during your day, noting the experience of shifting your awareness fully to the present moment through your environment.

- Practise **Box Breathing** for 5–10 minutes every day over a week. Note the effects of the regular practice.

- When next experiencing emotions, experiment with both mindfulness practices, as well as **Open Mindfulness of the Moment** (from Chapter 2) to anchor yourself in the refuge of this moment. Note how this works for you.

CHAPTER 6

Cultivating Grounding

Emotional storms can feel akin to being hijacked. When emotions are moving within our system many things are experienced simultaneously, as we've discussed in the chapters so far. Emotion is, in effect, an arousal, with challenging circumstances that may trigger the fight-or-flight reaction, a state of alarm in which emotions are a pivotal part. Our awareness and focus can easily be consumed by the emotional experience, the emotional reaction, and eclipse all else that is also present. This is usually not helpful for us, unless we are actually facing an immediately threatening and dangerous situation, where to fight, flee or freeze effectively preserves our life, and is a genuine priority.

In the previous key areas, the power of being present, mindful, in the here and now, as fully as possible, was explored. In this chapter we extend the power of being present to the particular concept and practice of 'grounding'—the cultivation of a deeper sense of being connected to the physical aspects of your world and being, in this moment, no matter what else may be happening.

BENEFITS OF GROUNDING

Grounding is about connection to the physical world as a primary resource. Through the practice of grounding, we can navigate our emotions more easily, regardless of the external surroundings we find ourselves in.

Availability 24 hours 7 days a week

The physical body is always in the present moment. It is a key asset in assisting us with a present-moment focus. The opportunity to relate to the physical body in a meaningful way and experience it through the five senses, is always available to us.

Supports a focus shift

The body can provide an anchor during strong emotions that helps to shift the emotional experience in a helpful, healthy way. By using awareness of the physical body, a complete focus on the emotions gets counterbalanced with a solid, stable reality: our physicality. The emotions are still present exactly as they are, but it is in the focus (where our attention is trained) that the shift happens. The sense of stability can effectively counterbalance any sense of emotional overwhelm.

Gaining a realistic perspective

Through grounding in the body, awareness broadens out and a naturally more accurate and realistic experience of the moment can gain traction. The action of broadening the focus beyond the emotions to the physical body and environment serves to put things into perspective. As seen through the fight-or-flight response, when a threat is perceived, all our attention and our system is primed towards the perceived threat. The view of the world can become very narrow; the negativity bias can take over. Grounding assists with challenging this.

Increasing the solid base

When one thinks of being in a storm, a central perceived risk and fear is being at the mercy of its dynamic forces, thrown about wildly by a storm's momentum—a loss of control and agency within yourself to counter the forces at play. Practising grounding assists in building resources to reduce the impact and retain some sense of both control and innate stability. Grounding is about increasing connection to a solid base of the earth and therefore, increasing this sense of solidness within, despite other factors and circumstances.

Interrupting emotional cycling

Clear recognition of the supports of the physical can reduce emotional cycling due to feelings of being unsupported. As part of secondary emotional reactions, a common inner compounding factor is the sense of feeling at the mercy of emotions, without support. Grounding can literally provide a shift in the alarm that this lack of support can trigger. Further, practising grounding validates ourselves as key players in cultivating our own stability and support, versus looking for it from others or external to us. It boosts a sense of agency and control.

KEY CONCEPT: Grounding

By **grounding**, we are not talking about being sent to your room because you were naughty. Nor are we referring to an in-depth understanding or knowledge in a topic such as, 'Susie had a solid grounding in online marketing strategies'. Both, however, do underline something of the sense of what grounding is: being in contact with something in a tangible, in-depth, solid, focused way.

THE BODY

The body is always present in the here and now, and it has weight and gravity as qualities. It also functions to facilitate a connection through the five senses to the world we inhabit. Being grounded to a large extent is about being in contact with the physical body, being 'embodied' and inhabiting the physicality we all possess.

BOUNDARIES

Through the sense of touch, the contact with the physical environment with our own physicality, we feel our own boundaries clearly. Literally, our personal boundaries are marked by our skin surface. It is through touch that we encounter the solidity upon which we rest—the earth, the ground, the contact of these with our feet and body.

Grounding means being connected to earth, feet on the ground, a sense of somatic, physical connection with the physical tangible world around us.

If we lack awareness of or lose our grounding, we risk struggling with strong emotional experiences. We risk missing out on tapping into something that aids us in realising our emotional truth and supports us as we inhabit this physical realm. We risk feeling unsupported and adrift.

AN IMPORTANT NOTE ON TRAUMA

A trauma background can create a legitimate resistance to grounding and feeling the physical body. Frequently, trauma experiences have occurred to or included the physical body. The body as a site of trauma absolutely needs to be respected.

A gentle approach is required that assists in rebuilding connection to the body that feels discreetly different to physical sensations associated with the trauma experience. Therefore, grounding practices might be through a certain 'safe' part of the body, they might be with a focus on external elements of a safe environment rather than a direct focus on the body itself.

The mindfulness exercise of **5-4-3-2-1 Senses Counting** is one such exercise that enhances grounding and allows for a safe controlled environment to be utilised for people with a trauma history (see Chapter 5).

Equally, past trauma experiences can continue to be felt as a sensitivity in and activation of the fight-or-flight system. Understanding this can be an important step in healing the impacts of the trauma as well as providing a framework for practising management skills with associated emotions.

Professional support for working with trauma is recommended to ensure the recovery work is paced in a safe, empowering way.

PATHWAYS TO INCREASED GROUNDING

The physical body offers many doorways into practising and building increased grounding. These approaches can be utilised as daily regular practices for balance and health, as well as intentionally practised during times when intense emotions and stress are experienced.

KEYS FOR PRACTICE

In setting out to practise ideas within this chapter here are a few general tips to remember:

- Practise during times of less emotion and stress within, to help gain experience with the practices, familiarity with what is being aimed for and experience with monitoring your own personal levels of grounding. By cultivating the practice no matter how you are feeling, they become easier to recall and put into play when emotion hits.
- Remember, when you are experiencing an emotional storm, it can be challenging to be mindful (understanding grounding as an extension of here and now present moment awareness) due to the impact of the emotions. Be realistic and remember that it is the intention to practise that matters.
- By developing healthy habits ahead of time, recall of them when they could be helpful, is increased.
- There is no right or wrong, achieving or failing: there is simply practice, launched from precisely where you are.
- Only you can experience grounding in your own body, so experimenting and noticing what happens is a key to realising when you are grounded or not—knowing innately what grounding feels like.

GROUNDING PRACTICES

We will focus on three directions or 'doorways' into the practice of grounding. They are:

- through the physical body and gravity
- through the physical body senses
- through structure and routines in daily life.

UTILISING THE PHYSICAL BODY AND GRAVITY

The word *grounding* points us towards the physical earth, and this first doorway into cultivating grounding is the direct use of the physical body and weight—gravity in action. In the contemporary, Western world, where many of us are freed from strong physical labour, it is easy to have missed developing familiarity with the body. Labour and transport, the two pivotal purposes of our body in days of old, has been relieved with technological advances. Movement and labour have become voluntary to a great degree for many in first world societies, the triumph of greater security and wealth. In the contemporary world, it is often through sport that the strongest bonds with our physical body are maintained.

The body has a weight and girth, a physicality with boundaries, edges and limits, experienced within space and our environment.

To cultivate grounding, the skills of mindfulness practice are employed. Grounding is a here and now experience. Awareness is needed to focus on the experience of being grounded. Awareness during all these practices requires inner sensing of the physical body.

This can include movements of the muscles, bones, joints, ligaments and tissue. It can also include the sensing of temperature and temperature changes in the body. Frequently such grounding awareness can also increase awareness of muscular tensions within the body and other aches and pains. This awareness is a positive thing: to note what is present and a reality for you physically right now. The power of awareness, with its in-built quality of acceptance, has its own magic in shifting challenging experiences.

PRACTICE POINT: Simple Grounding Exercise

Preparation: Stand with feet flat on the ground, roughly
                  shoulder width apart.
                  Have the feet generally parallel and pointing
                  straight ahead.
                  Allow the arms to hang from the shoulder sockets
                  loose and relaxed as possible.

Exercise: Gently bend the knees to lower the body towards
                  the ground.
                  Gently push up through the legs to almost
                  straighten the legs (allow knee joints to be
                  slightly bent, not locked).
                  This is a small movement to feel the weight of
                  the body and big thigh muscles engage; do not
                  do it like a fitness exercise and bend the knees too
                  dramatically.

See the diagram below. Repeat 5–10 times slowly.

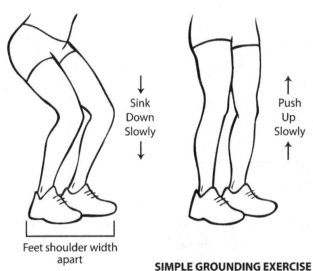

Sink
Down
Slowly

Push
Up
Slowly

Feet shoulder width
apart

SIMPLE GROUNDING EXERCISE

As you do this exercise, notice the physical sensation of the large leg muscles at work with the up and down movement. Notice the soles of the feet firm on the ground throughout the movement. Ensure you breathe naturally and do not unconsciously hold your breath.

THE LEGS, THE LEGS

In my years of practising mindfulness, of being aware of my grounding and how to enhance it, I have used walking with awareness of the feet and legs as a simple yet pivotal practice.

As an anxious kid who was overwhelmed a lot of the time out in the world and around other people, part of this package deal was a complete disconnect from being aware of and connected with my body. It was like I was in retreat, even within my own physicality, in a profound way—retreat from the edges completely, at all costs. Being ungrounded was the default setting, with no consciousness of what I was doing or of any different options available to me.

It went further than this—and I see it as a compounding of being disembodied—in that when I was asked to do something physical, I was afraid. I was resistant and afraid to be in the body. As you can imagine this invited a lot of emotional storms along the way.

Sports carnivals in particular were a nightmare for me. I was a redhead who was not allowed to play sport in the harsh summer sun, and, as could be the teaching style of the 70s, shamed by the sports teacher into solitude underneath a gum tree at the edge of the playground. Disembodied to boot.

However, there were rare moments during those early years when I had the wits about me to challenge this and the identity it gave me.

One day leading up to a sports carnival, I saw that the class was struggling to find people for the running relay. In some daredevil, adventurous moment I put my hand up. I could see that other kids were not top runners either, but they wanted to run. I decided I would too.

On the day, I just went for it, I ran in a way I had never tried before (and with no thought of training in the lead up to it, of course). It was a rare moment of breaking the mould and feeling the body fully, discomforts and all.

Afterwards, as I walked back to my sports team, a teacher said to me, 'Oh, I didn't know you were a good runner'. I smiled inside; I smiled outside. I felt empowered. I had burst forth from a very opposite kind of identity of myself. My team hadn't even won, we came last if I remember correctly. But I felt like a winner. I hadn't known I was a good runner either, because I had never tried.

How had I attained this as a totally new experience? I remember I just kind of owned my legs. I felt the power they were capable of, or I tested out the power they might be capable of. I allowed direct contact with them and off I went.

PRACTICE POINT: Zen Walking

The legs are our connection to a lower gravity centre in our bodies and with big, hard-working muscles, they offer a great focus for many forms of grounding work. Since that race, I have used my legs and feet for supporting myself when I might feel emotionally overwhelmed or I want to practise mindfulness. I discovered that having a clear contact with my physicality does give me a greater feeling of stability and resources to tap into, whatever the experience I am facing.

One of the regular ways I tune into grounding through awareness is when I walk. I first experienced mindful walking through a practice called Zen walking, as part of a silent sitting meditation retreat. Silent sitting sessions would end with a voluntary fifteen minutes of getting up, in silence, and doing slow Zen walking. This practice was to bring awareness and focus to the soles of the feet as you walked.

Instructions for Zen walking
- Walk with focus and awareness on the soles of the feet.
- Notice the connection to the ground and the movement of the feet as you take each step.

- Allow walking to slow down for increased mindfulness (but not so slow that you lose your balance).
- Let the eyes gaze softly towards the ground, unfocused as you walk.

UTILISING THE FIVE SENSES

Another major characteristic of our physiology is found in the five senses: sight, hearing, touch, taste and smell. These senses act as a kind of interface with our external environment as well as a means of monitoring activity within our internal world.

The next grounding practices focus on our sensual awareness as an anchor to our body and physicality. It also serves as an environmental anchor to the physical reality of the world around us.

PRACTICE POINT: Senses Walk

Choose a place to take a **Senses Walk**. This can be anywhere that is available and convenient. Doing this exercise invites openness to the world, so choose somewhere that feels attractive to you and safe emotionally. If possible, a nature setting is ideal as it can provide an appealing, safe environment to intentionally open up our senses, more than usual. For this exercise, opening of the senses requires anticipated relaxed environments. We are aiming very specifically to not engage the fight-or-flight system here.

Choose a frame for yourself to practise this:
- a set time for the walk (duration)
- or a set walking route (set path).

For example, I live in the inner city and there is a block of parkland on my street, with grass, trees and running water (as well as numerous running pooches). When I feel the need to ground myself and let go of stress, I might choose to go for a Senses Walk around the park.

I choose early morning or evening when it is quieter and less busy as this lends itself to opening up to the world, when there is less potential stimulation. I say to myself that I will circle the park three times, thus providing a frame for my walk. Personally, I tend to choose the set path so I don't need to try and keep track of time during the walk, which can be distracting.

If choosing a time duration, experiment with using an alarm on your mobile phone or smart watch to alert you to the time.

Senses Walk instructions:
- As I walk, I bring my awareness to all my senses.
- I allow myself to open them up and experience them as I move.

While walking this includes tactile sensing of any breeze or wind, sensing the temperature, of direct sunlight on my skin or of cool shadow, the sense of my body physically moving, including the impact of each footstep through my body.

Through the sense of hearing, I become aware of any surrounding sounds within the environment. These can include sounds of my own body walking, bird sounds, wind, cars, people, etc. Smells can be subtle or stronger depending upon your environment but may include smells of nature such as flower perfume, the smell of rain, and other smells such as food. Taste tends to be the lesser sense generally unless you are eating.

Connection to the physical world
Another way to experience grounding is beyond our bodies through physical contact with things in our environment, via our senses.

PRACTICE POINT: Belly to Earth
Choose a natural setting, ideally with grass.

Lie face down in a comfortable position with your head turned to one side. Allow the whole front of the body to be in contact with the ground. Arms can be at your side or stretched outwards, palms down in contact with the earth where possible.

103

Feel the sensation of the contact of your body with the earth. Notice the belly area as a kind of centre for your whole-body perception. Allow yourself to simply be with this moment, taking in the physical sensation of belly to earth.

Allow the breath to be easy and natural.

PRACTICE POINT: Hug a Tree

Yes, I mean it, have you ever hugged a tree?

Do you associate it with greenies and protesters seeking to prevent logging?

Well, how about we bring this concept back to the actual *isness* of hugging a tree and in true mindfulness style, allow associations to be there but focus on the sensory experience that comes with hugging a tree. Suspend judgement and self-consciousness and try it. I can vouch for the fact that it is awesome and provides a very unique opportunity to be in the here and now moment, opening up the senses, particularly of touch and smell, and allowing feeling in a safe, simple manner.

As with lying face down on the ground and connecting with the earth, we instead remain standing and bring our arms around the base of a solid, old tree trunk. Hug it as you would someone that you feel relaxed with and care about.

UTILISING ROUTINE AND STRUCTURE

A different direction to assist with grounding is using daily routines and structure in your life. Routine and structure assist us to increase our grounding, feeling ourselves within a frame, held and supported. Structure and routine provide us with a solid base to rest on, to lean into and fall back on.

While not physical as such, structure provides a mental, psychological solidity. I have noted how it has assisted me in increasing the feeling of groundedness in my life from a very different yet equally effective approach.

In supporting people who experience depression and anxiety regularly in my practice, the use of structure and routine is a significant resource for daily living and coping.

With any strong emotions, turning to routines and structures in your day that support essential self-care, activities, functions and basic securities of life (such as work, parenting, maintaining health, meeting responsibilities, etc.) provides a stable, secured base during emotionally challenging times. Structure and routine offer something to pour your energy and attention into that holds neutral or positive benefits as a way of managing times of emotional challenge and uncertainty.

KEY CONCEPT: Structure and Routine

Structure means something arranged and organised with a clear, asserted pattern. Examples of this in life include a work schedule or sectioning off different parts of the day for different tasks and focuses. Structure in daily life has a distinct temporal nature to it: structuring time.

Routine means a regular course or procedure that is habitual or established. It can cross over with structuring the day or week, but it also refers to established procedures that are included in daily life. Examples of different types of routines include self-care routines, maintaining or 'getting healthy' routines, work routines, getting ready for work routines, or different times of the day, such as morning and evening routines.

Committing to a structure or activity for a time period, can contain the energy that might otherwise get swept up and consumed by uncontained thinking and emotion. As we have seen, during emotional storms the emotional process can certainly dominate and often completely consume a person, in the feelings themselves and associated thoughts and behaviours. A structure or routine provides a place to focus energy, distracts from focusing on the emotion within, and provides a holding frame to rest in when feeling unsettled.

Thus, it feels supportive.

Choosing a structure or routine that does not feel overwhelming or daunting is important. As with all goal setting (and this is a type of goal setting) it needs to be achievable. Try to get the level of commitment right. One of the ways in which this strategy can falter is by choosing structure or a routine that creates emotions through the stress and high demand of a chosen task.

When I realise I am in stormy weather and want to support myself through structure, I choose something very approachable, even one activity at a time. If I am experiencing intense emotions I might think about a structure or routine for the next couple of hours that supports me while processing the feeling. And then after the few hours, usually with emotion having shifted, I can look at the next segment of my day.

Typical personal examples of structure and routine when feeling emotion include:

- Household tasks: wash the bedsheets, put on a load of washing, tidy the kitchen or bathroom, cook healthy food for a few meals ahead (including going shopping for ingredients)
- Complete a walk for an hour
- Play my musical instrument for half an hour, or commit to several music pieces and scales to practise
- Decide to have a warm bath and listen to music or a podcast.

REFLECTION POINT

Note any current routines that you incorporate into your day that may support your emotional wellbeing and management. Take a moment now to clearly identify and take stock of structure and routines in your life that you draw on already.

Create a list of possible structures and routines that you can easily access in the future. Have a collection of at least five possibilities on your list.

PRACTICE POINT: Structure and Routine

The next time you identify being in the midst of emotion, experiment with choosing some form of structure and routine to try for an hour. Notice the before and after-effects on your emotional self.

Please note: in the spirit of mindfulness, all of the approaches to grounding and different exercises presented include space for feelings to be present exactly as they are, without directly focusing on them. All approaches are designed to be done mindfully and support emotional processing through allowing feelings while cultivating grounding in your body and world.

IN SUMMARY

The practice of grounding helps reduce emotional storms and stress through increasing our sense of a solid, extended foundation upon which we rest.

Despite turbulence and real, legitimate challenges, intentionally placing awareness on our physical body reminds us of the physical body as a resource—something tangible—that we can draw on as a stabilising force.

We can cultivate grounding through our connection to our weight and gravity through legs and feet, through our five senses, through tactile contact with our environment, and through resting in routines and structures.

With past trauma experiences, grounding needs to be approached in a sensitive way, often supported by working with a trained trauma-informed mental health professional (a counsellor, psychologist, psychiatrist, therapist or social worker).

TAKEAWAY PRACTICES

When you next notice emotions within, check on your sense of your feet on the ground and try one of the below exercises to increase your grounding:

- **Simple Grounding Exercise**

- **Zen Walking**

- **Senses Walk**

- **Belly to the Earth**

- **Hug a Tree**

- **Create a Structure for the Day**

- **5-4-3-2-1 Senses Counting** (Chapter 3).

CHAPTER 7

Habits, Habits, Habits

A s human beings we are all creatures of habit by our very design. We create automatic 'shortcuts' that get us through our day and life, often with barely a thought about what we are doing.

Habits are the result of the way that our brains work and involve cognitions (or thinking) as well as emotions. These internal processes then flow into an action or behaviour, that becomes routine and regularly enacted (the habit itself). This behaviour or action in turn creates an outcome or consequence.

Habits are about creating an outcome that we regard as positive, to achieve a status better than what we started with. Often, shifting our feelings is a major part of the desired change that our habits target.

Looking at how some of our habits are entwined with changing or moderating our mood and emotional state is helpful. This key focuses on the emotional dimensions that come along with habits and that can be part of the fabric of some habit processes that we identify as not effective or helpful.

Some examples of habits with clear emotional content can be:
- eating when feeling stressed, sad, angry or bored
- exercising religiously to try to feel attractive enough
- smoking a cigarette when feeling anxious or bored
- going to the pub to avoid boredom or loneliness
- avoiding social situations to feel less scared and ashamed, as this is what contact with people stirs up
- seeking someone to talk out problems to alleviate stress every time stress is there, as it feels too overwhelming alone.

In these examples, actions become repeated or routine 'go-to' habits, to try to change challenging emotions.

However, habits can also support emotional health and effective living, tapping into attending to physical, social and psychological needs that contribute to emotional wellness.

Examples include:
- drinking water first thing every morning
- taking the stairs instead of the lift
- phoning a friend or family member regularly, to stay in touch and connected
- taking care of yourself through routinely bathing, cleaning your house, taking out the garbage, decluttering once a year, grooming and dressing yourself in certain ways.

A second focus of this key area centres on direct emotional habits— baseline habits around the feelings we feel.

Examples of this could include routinely:
- crying when angry
- feeling fearful when no current reason to feel afraid
- withholding or hiding our feelings
- feeling unworthy around people
- not allowing anger, sadness, jealousy, irritation
- dismissing feelings within

- judging feelings when they arise
- not being allowed to feel excited
- feeling shame around showing feelings
- being emotionally expressive and unable to contain emotions
- feeling dominated by one particular feeling when feelings begin to arise
- feeling shame around positive feelings towards oneself
- allowing certain emotions and not others.

Such emotional habits—the automatic way we deal with emotions arising within, by replacing feelings, or reverting to a common 'baseline' emotion—can narrow our emotional experience and sense of what is really occurring within. The range of our feeling responses can become narrow and less effective if something automatic kicks in, versus responding to the present emotional reality afresh. With this type of habit, expressions of feeling become habitual and the truth of the emotional experience gets subverted in some way.

But first, let's have a look at what a habit is ...

KEY CONCEPT: Defining a Habit

A **habit** represents a cognitive shortcut we set in motion repeatedly. It is driven by the evolutionary goal of increased effectiveness, without the need to keep cognitively processing (or thinking about) the same or similar situations, every time we encounter them. Habits bypass thinking on many levels, and are designed to enhance our performance of familiar, frequent life tasks and responses to circumstances.

Within the brain, the more advanced capacity to think, reflect and analyse is bypassed with habits. If the habit is formed it becomes a neurological reality—within the brain, the shortcut becomes a physical pathway through the brain cells, literally akin to a well-worn pathway. Taking the habit pathway therefore becomes automatic in nature because it is literally a common and easily accessible route and habits are strengthened by repetition.

Conditions for setting up habits include:

- A stable environment in which the habit takes place (familiar, consistent)
- Repetition of circumstances requiring a response (the situation the habit is a response to or solution for).

Habits are often given a negative wrap in the media with a focus on unhealthy habits that people commonly struggle to change (such as some of the examples given previously).

However, ultimately, habits are the neutral potential of our human brains and developing them is inevitable. They can fulfil their purpose of saving us time and creating effective shortcuts. They can be harnessed for wellbeing and optimal functioning. It is the consequences of these habits and what they achieve, that is important. Deciding what is 'healthy' often comes down to function (how functional the habit ends up being) and key questions to begin constructive enquiry are listed below.

The Four Basic Questions

- Does this habit work?
- Does this habit achieve what I am trying to achieve?
- Is there some physical addictiveness or compulsivity at play in the enacting out of this habit?
- Do I have the capacity to choose rather than act automatically when desired?

This chapter is about reviewing our habits and noting the emotional motivations and outcomes of them, where relevant. We will all have habits (or automatic programs) running around our emotional experiences. During emotional storms, times of high emotional intensity or challenging emotions, habits can kick in. Tips for understanding and assessing your habits, for working with functional, healthy habits, for reducing or replacing unhealthy, dysfunctional habits are presented.

ACTING AUTOMATICALLY

Habits have an automatic quality to them. A classic, oft-cited example of the way habits kick in and run automatically, can be found with driving.

People get behind the wheel of their car, set off, driving towards a familiar destination, and reach there as planned, often with no actual memory of how they got there. They were busy thinking about other things, but just kept driving according to the well-worn, familiar route and a well-honed familiarity with how to operate a car. In this example the car is the stable, familiar environment for this particular habit to play out.

I have certainly ended up at places that I wasn't intending to go as I followed a well-worn path, thinking and busily focused on other things besides driving, such as what happened at work, people in my life, pressing demands on me, and other life matters. I forgot that I was not actually going to work, I was trying to go somewhere else; or when I had two jobs, that I was going to one workplace and not the other. Let us just say that tolls have been paid unnecessarily and time has been spent in traffic that could have been avoided.

HABITS AS WAYS OF COPING

Habits represent a means of coping with the demands we experience from both our external and internal environs. It is a way of seeking to function effectively, even though we may recognise that it does not actually achieve this sometimes.

Habits that are linked in with emotions often are habitualised attempts to cope with difficult and challenging repeated emotions and emotion-producing situations. They can be routine strategies to cope when the fight-or-flight system gets triggered.

Common actions towards painful emotions that may become habitual include:

- to avoid
- minimise
- to attack or fight with

- to push away
- to deaden or numb.

Equally, as noted in previous chapters, we may develop habits around commonly desired emotions such as happiness, confidence, self-love and pride. This may involve unworthiness or fear to feel good in and about oneself; or alternatively, holding onto positive feelings in a controlling, unrealistic way, in a desire to have them continue.

Other common actions that become habitual may include:
- to cling to
- to reject
- to feel secondary feelings like anxiety or fear.

REFLECTION POINT

Take a moment right now to list five of your habits. Try not to censor or judge them as 'good or bad'. Simply write down habits you identify as part of the fabric of your daily life.

Now notice how easy or difficult that was for you to do. Notice any preconceived ideas and a focus on habits as problems. We are simply looking for repeated, regular shortcuts taken in your life.

The ones that I came up with this morning included:

- coffee at a café first thing every morning
- checking my keys are in my hand before I close the front door
- eating in front of the TV
- trying to please people without often checking in with myself
- overcommitting with projects, taking a lot on.

Now reflect on your five habits and their automatic nature, how they may operate as a coping mechanism, for emotional content, and apply The Four Basic Questions to consider how they work for you in your life.

Please note: Only you can assess whether a habit is positive or negative for you, or in-between. What works for one person can be different to what works for another. Equally, what you decide is effective and functional for you is yours alone to decide, and not to be compared with anyone else's version of truth. You are the one who ultimately passes assessment on what you do and what you decide to do about what you do!

In exploring this chapter allow all kind of habits to float up within your awareness; there will be both effective and ineffective habits, functional and dysfunctional shortcuts that we live out through our habits.

BENEFITS OF EXAMINING OUR HABITS

Awareness brings change

Habits are automatic and often unconsciously driven; they can feel as if they develop a life and momentum of their own. By bringing in awareness and genuinely recognising patterns of habitual behaviours and thinking that involve our emotions, our perspective can shift. As underlined throughout this book, presence and awareness are incredibly powerful.

By shining the light of awareness on habits built around our emotions and emotional selves, linked to regulating or managing our emotions, we see them more clearly for what they are. Change can occur when something is fully recognised and understood.

Open up options

Awareness provides us with a very different position from which to act.

Once we see that what we repeat automatically does not serve us anymore, we have the option of replacing it with a more productive and potentially healthier way of responding. We have the possibility to stop acting in ways we do not actually want.

This is important with common addictive habits such as overeating, smoking or use of substances. Awareness brings in the shift from reacting in a habitual, automatic way to responding in a conscious way.

Genuinely attending to emotional needs

When habits are centred on responding to repeated emotional needs, often the positive consequence is short term—short term relief, reprieve, distraction, avoidance, comfort, soothing, mood boost or deadening of unwanted feelings. By becoming aware of habits tied in with emotion management, we can revisit the effectiveness of what we do and how we feel. It provides an opportunity to better understand our emotions and to then respond in a healthy, often more direct and fulfilling way to the need they represent.

If we continue to allow emotional habits to kick-in automatically, we will always respond the same, potentially in a 'blind' way that interferes with seeing each life situation for what it is. We can miss opportunities in the present.

THE HABIT CYCLE

Understanding the process of a habit in play can be helpful and aids in making conscious the oft-unconscious, automatic behaviour that habits represent.

The moving parts of **the habit cycle** include:

THE HABIT CYCLE

The cue: This is what triggers the habit, found either in the external or internal environment and suggests a reward to be had. Examples of a cue can be finishing work, coming home, hopping in the car, feelings arising such as anxiety, loneliness, fear, a time of the day (early morning, afternoon, night-time), or a repeated situation. Here the stable environment is part of the cue.

The motivation: This is the motivation or desire to act—there has to be a craving for change, a craving for something, that the habit seemingly promises to deliver in response to the cue. Examples of motivation can be to change an uncomfortable feeling to a more pleasant one or to deaden feelings, to improve a situation, to achieve an outcome, to reduce stress and demand, or to relax.

The action: This is performing the actual habit, taking action from the cue and the motivation stimulus to perform the habit. This is the regular, routine, repeated action that is the habit itself.

The reward: This is the outcome or consequence achieved by enacting the habit. It is often experienced as a kind of reward and can be associated with the release of a neurotransmitters such as dopamine, within the brain chemistry. Some habits do not necessarily deliver the promised 'reward' and this can be the set-up with addictions and compulsions. Or the reward can be short-lived, in direct relation to short-term dopamine and other neurotransmitter release, that does not provide an effective resolution of the motivation or craving in a sustainable way.

How does this look in real life?

REFLECTION POINT

Choose a habit and reflect on each of the parts of **the habit cycle** in the following way:

- Give the habit a name

- The cue is (name the common situation or circumstance, including environment).......

- The motivation is (name the craving or desire that gives the habit its momentum or fuel)......

- The action is (name the behaviour that is the actual habit)......

- The reward is (name the outcome or consequence gained through the habit).....

EMOTIONS AND HABITS

Any habit can have elements of emotion within them as a pivotal part of the process. And even healthy, effective and functional habits affect us emotionally, and can be part of management of our emotional selves and wellbeing.

For one, habits are familiar, and this familiarity in itself can provide a sense of comfort and security—whether effective or not, whether healthy and functional or not. Habits also can provide helpful supports during times of emotional storms through providing a channel for taking action of some kind, to relieve inner tension and to feel like you are 'doing something'. Enacting habits in this way can prove easy as habits are readily accessible. They can give a momentary sense of seeming control.

We all will have habits around our emotions—our 'style', our 'go to' behaviours, thoughts and beliefs that automatically occur when we have a feeling.

Within the habit cycle, emotion can often be part of the trigger or stimulus to do the habit (the motivation) as well as within the result of enacting the habit (the reward or consequence).

Consider the examples in the following table:

Habits, Habits, Habits

Cue	Motivation	Action	Reward	End result
Mike arrives home after a usual busy, stressful day at work	Mike wants to relax and reward himself	Mike lights up a cigarette and sits out on his balcony	The cigarette gives Mike a moment to stop and relax, free of the stress of work	Coming home and having a cigarette becomes associated with relaxing after work and being free
Linda finds herself alone and feeling lonely	Linda doesn't want to feel the loneliness and secondary emotion of sadness	Linda goes out to a shopping centre even though she has no errands or tasks to do there	Being out in public around other people alleviates the lonely feelings and distracts Linda	Every time Linda feels lonely, she immediately goes to the shops
Martha has had a baby and feels overwhelmed and everything seems out of control when at home	Martha needs to feel in control and that she is a 'good mother' and coping with her life	Martha begins to compulsively clean her house or be preoccupied with the idea of cleaning to demonstrate coping and control of her life through her home environment	When the house gets cleaned Martha regains a sense of control and that she is managing	Cleaning becomes a preoccupation in Martha's mind and she feels a constant need to try to clean to feel less stressed and in control

REFLECTION POINT

In each of these examples consider how the emotional content sits mostly within the cue and reward areas. Think about possible substitute actions that could be alternatives to meeting the emotional need.

HABITS AND CHANGE

Habits can endure lifelong, or may be acquired, changing throughout our lifetime. They can represent things that are helpful and assist us, represent things that we actually deride pleasure from and enjoyment doing, or they can be problematic, representing behaviour that we wish we could change (and often try to unsuccessfully) that have negative consequences.

Addictions and compulsive behaviour can be included within this habit category. Addictions often have a physical reality and dependence to them that makes change more complex and this is important to fully recognise and consider in attempts to change. Examples of addictions can be using substances including both illicit drugs and prescription medication, as well as alcohol and certain food.

Compulsivity means a heightened need or compulsion to do something that may relate to seeking to manage anxiety. Examples of compulsions can be to shoplift, shop excessively, gamble, eat or exercise excessively, or to do a certain behaviour before leaving the house. With both addiction and compulsions, professional input and assessment is highly recommended due to their complexity.

TIPS FOR WORKING WITH OUR HABITS

Use of awareness and slowing down the act

Through practising awareness—mindfulness of the moment, to everything present—we directly undermine the automatic quality of a habit. We seek to make conscious the unconscious shortcut that we have established through repetition. Through applying awareness, we also slow down the process. This slowing down through awareness immediately begins to shift and disrupt the habit. As stated previously throughout this book, presence and awareness hold an innate 'superpower' to instil change.

When people try to change a habit they frequently say, 'It happened so quickly that I didn't get a chance to do anything differently'. Yes, it is true that habits with strong emotional ties, with compulsive and addictive traits, can be very pervasive and relentless. Emotional reactions (the motivations or cravings) can fire off quickly and automatically.

A first step is to see the habit, to recognise it as clearly as possible, as it is happening. Even though you may still be doing an undesired act, the seeing of it is extremely important and offers an immediate opportunity for difference.

This is opposite to the often travelled path of trying to control and change the habit through willpower and grit. In resisting the habit and fighting against it, a secondary emotional reaction is often created, intensifying the emotional state.

Rather than creating an inner battle as so easily can occur, the second helpful step is to give yourself permission to slow things down … permission to press the pause button, again at any point that is possible. So you are not resisting or fighting with the habitual impulse fuelled by strong emotion, but rather you simply breathe space into it, slow things down, experiment with simply pausing. No avoidance, no fighting, no stress need be created.

Notice the habit kick-in, notice the urge to act, the impulse, the craving and motivation, the action of the habit and the outcome or consequences. Bring awareness to the habit at any point—but be aware!

The third step after slowing down and practising gentle pauses is to do something different, try something new. It will feel foreign at first but that is okay. Part of why we stick with habits is that they feel familiar, they have a certain comfort even if they may be to our detriment.

SURFING THE URGE

G. Alan Marlatt developed the famous urge surfing approach to working with addiction and relapse prevention. The urge to act out a habit—the motivation— tends to rise and fall, like a wave in the ocean. It builds momentum and intensity, rising to a peak, and then slowly subsides as the wave crest turns and dissipates, as shown in the diagram below.

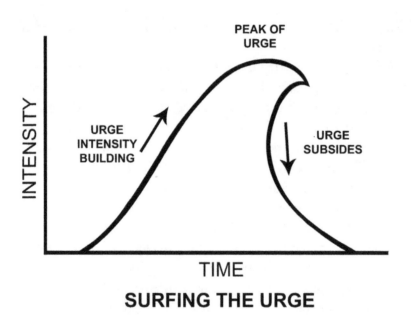

SURFING THE URGE

The Surfing the Urge approach offers a mindfulness-based practice of having impulses and urges, yet not needing to act on them. Instead we observe the experience of this wave and of the urge within.

PRACTICE POINT: Surfing the Urge

When a habit impulse is triggered, choose to 'sit' with the wave of the urge as it moves through the different stages.

Be alert and aware to all aspects of the urge wave: body sensations, thoughts, feelings, alongside the urges to act.

Allow the whole experience to be there as much as possible, neither feeding nor avoiding the process. Note judgements and beliefs; note the rise in intensity and the lessening of intensity when that occurs.

It can take practice to understand that it is okay to sit in a high energy state without acting on urges to take a certain action. Instead, observe.

THE CONSEQUENCES SCALE

In working with many people over the years, habits that people identify as destructive—addictions, activities that impact on health negatively, habits of avoidance, habitual responses that negatively affect relationships—are key issues presented during therapy.

A main way I have clients begin to view their unwanted habits or repeated patterns of emotional reaction, is through tracing the consequences of these habits.

Identifying consequences and assessing their impact in life and on wellbeing can be utilised to build awareness. It promotes understanding of automated behaviours, bringing consciousness to the intended outcome of them versus actual consequences. Looking at habits in this way assists in reviewing the effectiveness of the coping mechanisms we employ.

With this consequences scale, habits and coping mechanisms can be placed along a spectrum according to the outcomes they produce.

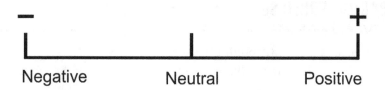

Negative   Neutral   Positive

The Consequences Scale

The three markers along the scale are:
- **negative outcomes** (the habit does not help but in fact makes things worse for me and contributes to my problems, has destructive outcomes to my health and/or relationships, harms me and others, and my ability to function in my life)
- **neutral outcomes** (the habit neither causes harm nor benefit BUT it does not add to my problems)
- **positive outcomes** (the habit creates improvement across health, wellbeing, relationships, tackling challenges and functioning in life).

It can also be helpful to think about timeframe with consequences.

How does the outcome change over the short term or immediate experience versus the medium term and long term?

For example, eating sweet foods may give immediate comfort and pleasure during times of stress and anxiety, but over the longer term create weight issues that affect both physical health and self-esteem.

A general rule of thumb is to look to the longer term, as habits (as repeated actions) have an accumulative effect on us and our lives.

It can also be helpful to understand that any habit or coping mechanism can be over-used or under-used, each throwing out the fine balance struck between healthy and unhealthy habits.

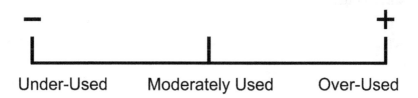

Rate of Use

> **REFLECTION POINT**
>
> Here are some questions and discussion points around using the scales of consequences and rate of use:
>
> - Where would I place the consequences or outcome of my habit along the consequences scale? Begin to seek out 'replacement habits' for negative outcomes that include a number of options.
>
> - If negative or neutral, can I think of other actions I could take to have as replacement or substitute options? Have a range of neutral and positive strategies on standby to begin to break a habitual response that you identify as wanting to change.
>
> - Note any over-use of one habit, under-use of others, and strive for multiple options instead of relying on a singular main habit. Plot habits along the scale according to frequency of use.
>
> - Develop healthy, responsive habits when we feel emotions, that rate as neutral or positive on the scale.
>
> - Replace scripted, old, outdated responses that kick-in automatically, where possible.

HABITS FOR EMOTIONAL RESILIENCE AND WELLBEING

In looking at habits, it is also important to recognise and affirm ones that support emotional wellbeing and health. As seen in the grounding chapter, routines can provide numerous benefits and be the fabric of effective, achievable self-care habits.

A habit can be a consciously chosen routine or practice that you actively work towards becoming a habit through the magic of repetition. It can take time to actively cultivate habits that you know work for you, building your sense of emotional wellbeing. They can be connected to physical health, with much-proven links with our emotional balance and mood.

Please note: When changing a habit, it can initially take time to feel the reward of the new action. In particular, with addictions and compulsive habits that generate the dopamine response, a replacement action may not feel as effective or rewarding.

The 'instant gratification' of the well-worn habit will not necessarily be there with the replacement action. It can take time to feel; it can be a different, less exciting reward compared to using substances and other behaviours.

It is important to be realistic in expectations and hold faith that the reward sought may come in a different and less intense form with more grounded and healthy practices. The reward may take a little time to adjust to and appreciate. It does not mean that the new habit is not working.

IN SUMMARY

Habits form the fabric of much of our everyday life. Habit formation is designed to create shortcuts in regular actions and circumstances, via creation of neural pathways bypassing normal 'one-off' thinking processes. The emotional dimensions to habits include the motivations to initiate the habit and the change that we seek through the habit. Often this change is a desired reward with significant emotional weight. We can also form habits as a way of seeking to handle emotions and create desired emotional shifts within. Habits can be a key part of maintaining wellbeing and self-care consciously.

TAKEAWAY PRACTICES

- Practise mindfulness of habits to build awareness around repeated automatic behaviours that involve emotions.

- Practise **Surfing the Urge** as developed by G. Alan Marrat.

- Break down a habit to its 'moving parts', identifying the cue, motivation, action or habit behaviour and reward. Then summarise the logic of the habit or function of the habit.

- Note the emotion points of a habit, often around the cue and reward. Work out what the emotional needs and attempts to cope are.

- Rate habit consequences on the consequences scale, making a realistic assessment of the outcomes of the habit being negative, neutral or positive for you. Brainstorm other actions that could address the emotional needs in a more effective way, with neutral or positive consequences. Try to come up with multiple options to try.

- Cultivate habits that support your emotional health and wellbeing, and begin to enact them in your daily routine. Be realistic about the time needed to reap the rewards of new habits.

CHAPTER 8

Relationship to Self

Our relationship with our self is intimately linked to our relationship with our emotional self—how we regard our emotions and the experiences they provide us. This relationship with self also has direct bearing on the kind of emotions we experience. If we do not feel positively towards ourselves, if we actively judge and criticise ourselves as a person and for our emotions, this will usually generate many more challenging emotional states. As previously noted, secondary emotional reactions are a real phenomenon that can complicate and escalate emotional storms within. Feelings about our self are a prime area where such challenging secondary emotions can occur for a variety of reasons.

Learned attitudes about our feelings set us up for and contribute to our feelings about who we are. Comparison to others—differences in how we may look, our vulnerabilities and strengths, our temperament and expression—directly feed into our relationship to self.

In this chapter, the relationship to self is explored as vital to understanding, navigating and embracing emotional experience. The central aim of this key area is to check in on your feelings towards yourself.

Such feelings may tap into issues of worthiness, capacity to value yourself, love and liking for oneself, self-compassion, and the capacity to tune into, take care of and meet one's own needs. It taps into how you may automatically treat yourself. It also offers ways of improving this relationship and actions that can affirm your inherent value. This in turn can facilitate improved feelings towards yourself, which flows into improved emotional states.

Female, red hair, emotional

From early on in life—around age four—I quickly developed a sense that I was 'too emotional', to such a point that 'emotional' became a core quality of my fledgling identity. Our identity is based on 'knowledge' of ourselves and much is derived from the feedback we receive from the world around us. Many of my earliest identity-gathering experiences revolved around this issue of being 'too sensitive' and 'too emotional'.

I recall being frequently emotionally overwhelmed, flooded with sensations and feelings—literally in emotional storms. Many scenarios and situations simply felt too much for me at that time. They were usually when I was required to step out into the wider world beyond the familiar safety of home, around new situations such as school, social events and unknown people. And with the sudden rush of feeling 'too much' would come tears and feeling emotionally flooded, unable to speak up, choked up with a multitude of feelings. And then would come the refrain from others: 'You are so sensitive' or 'You are very emotional'.

It was a neat vicious cycle and resulted in developing a negative perception of emotion generally and of my emotional self from early on. My identity began to form closely around this quality, of being emotional as a core trait of who I was, alongside the other two central ones—female and a redhead. Emotional, female, redhead.

Even at such a young age, I implicitly picked up that my emotion was problematic to others, that it seemed different to other people's version of emotionality. Being emotional was stressful—frequent emotional storms, feeling overwhelmed and seemingly at the mercy of difficult feelings, then criticised for something I could not seem to control.

It *was* true that I was emotionally sensitive and open, that I seemed to experience feelings intensely, just being in my own skin. The struggle was real; however, it was the only 'normal' I knew, and emotional sensitivity and feeling were key traits of mine as a person, without question.

In time, as I got older, an upside began to emerge. I began to pour the feeling into creative ventures where I found a nonverbal, immediate, and real outlet for all my emotion. In going to school there were many creative opportunities in the early years, and this sensitivity suddenly found legs in allowing me to be alert to things in my own unique way and expressing them with purpose. Over time my budding identity began to shift from merely 'emotional' to 'emotional and artistic and talented'.

It was a definite improvement and the way I felt about myself and my emotions began to shift.

Creativity proved an ongoing theme throughout my early years into adulthood, and has been an essential lifeline throughout my life, particularly at times when words did not seem to do justice to the emotions within: during the years when my family was under the shadow of two family members missing; after my father died and I was back at boarding school; and at other times when I needed to feel myself in a solid way, that nothing else seemed to offer.

The positive side of being emotionally open and sensitive to emotions generally was not a strength or asset until I began to find my creativity. It also however led me to reassess and critically question how my early life set-up had left me with myself.

The relationship with myself had an automatic negative attitude to my emotions—a dismissal and rejection of my emotions, which in turn produced its own compounding issues. I was rejecting a core part of myself rather than being able to be with it and see it for what it was. Through working on my own relationship with myself, things began to shift dramatically. And one of the key first steps was becoming conscious and alert to the fact that I had a relationship with myself.

THE CONCEPT OF RELATIONSHIP

Relationships and relating are core to our very existence and the life we lead. Using the concept of 'relationship' can be very enlightening when we think about it in regard to ourselves.

We all know what the word *relationship* means with other people and that tends to be how we think about relationships in our life—relationship *to* others.

KEY CONCEPT: Defining Relationship

Relationship can be defined as the way in which two or more people or things are connected, or the state of being connected.

All relationships share certain features that help define the nature of them.

Within the connection, such features to be aware of can include:
- the level of care and respect
- the attitude or overall 'take' on the other in the relationship
- degrees of intimacy or closeness
- degrees of positive, negative or indifferent regard
- degrees of honesty
- degrees of flexibility
- behaviour towards each other.

There is also the degree of attachment, if any, and this concept will be explored further in the following chapter.

Variations of relationships

We certainly experience a vast array of different types of relationships, with different levels of emotional connection and intimacy, that serve varying functions in our life and roles. The context of meeting—or the way we have come to know each other—can also moderate the nature of the relationship:

- Is it personal? As with a friend, partner, sibling, parent, child?
- Is it another kind of defined role like work that is not personal? Is it as a customer, patient or client?
- Is it a 'blood' connection within family that brings with it a host of particular expectations and ideals?
- Is it a community connection that is embedded in culture or faith?

These contexts all influence the nature of connections between people through the rules of engagement established that lie beyond the personal, tapping into cultural and social expectations and norms.

Other factors that we take in as we formulate the relationship with another person include the physicality of the person, their character and personal qualities, their attitudes and emotional bearing, their behaviour and the way they regard us.

The more we care about a relationship, the more emotion is usually present in the connection. Affection gives a tone to relationships as a whole and determines the potential importance and significance each has for us. All these factors can drive our overall behaviour towards the other, our approach to them and the emotional regard held within that particular connection.

And, in the same way as we think about relationship with others, so too can we think about our relationship with ourselves.

For this key area, for reading this chapter and appreciating the significance of this to your emotional reality, I want you to turn your gaze 180° degrees, towards yourself.

ME, MYSELF AND I

The relationship we have with our self is real, incredibly significant and in operation all the time—waking or sleeping. It sets up a whole ripple effect on how we behave in the world: the expectations we hold for ourselves in life, the hopes and options we see as possible for ourselves. Our relationship to our self and the emotions involved in that also communicate themselves to other people, often in indirect, unspoken ways.

Thus, there are real, substantial consequences to the way we relate with ourselves, contributing significantly to how we show up in our life. This in turn results in generating or triggering emotions and setting an emotional tone within, as a direct consequence of how our inner relationship influences and sets us up in life.

As in all relating, there can be healthy and unhealthy types of relationships, destructive or constructive types of connections, harmonious or conflictual feelings, and these can mark what flows out of our relationship to self, into what happens within our lives. Emotions are an integral part of the story we hold about ourselves and the story we tell others—how we account for who we are as a person. Whether these stories are real and accurate or not, whether they are unhealthy and destructive, or healthy and helpful, is another dimension. And within all of this, we each have an active role to play in our relationship to self, making key and powerful choices around what we do with what is within our control.

To make conscious and clear the status of our relationship to self brings considerable benefits.

BENEFITS IN CHECKING ON OUR RELATIONSHIP WITH OURSELVES

Seeing clearly what is

Firstly, as we have seen previously, awareness assists in seeing clearly what is. Reality is a great place to start—in fact, it is the only place we have to start— and anything is possible if we are clear about where we truly are. Awareness aids us in challenging unhelpful, unkind, inaccurate feelings towards ourselves, that do not serve us in life. Awareness helps us identify default positions towards ourselves that are judgemental and antagonistic.

Opportunity to challenge unhelpful attitudes

Once we can see any habitual patterns in how we treat ourselves, only then can we question and challenge any negative ideas we enact.

If we bring consciousness to how we currently feel about and treat ourselves, we create the opportunity to behave differently. Consciousness and awareness create a climate for change by their very nature. I certainly experienced this when it was pointed out to me how judgemental and critical of myself I was.

Intellectually it made sense that without positive feeling towards myself life could be an ongoing misery and no doubt never feel 'right' to me. If I did not respect or like myself … and it was *my* life that I was living … well it was just bound to be difficult. It also helped that someone respectfully pulled me up on this. By their very questioning of this automatic way of my being with myself, I got the message that it was okay to respect and care for self, in a meaningful, deliberate way.

Reduce challenging emotions

Without cultivating an ability to love, respect and value oneself, to feel the opposite, provides fertile ground for negative feelings about yourself and your life to continue to proliferate. It sets up a cascade of difficult feelings a lot of the time, a compounding effect as you move through your days, encountering incidents that point to your own worth.

By consciously developing positive feelings and a healthy relationship to self, difficult emotions that are founded on self-judgement naturally shrink.

HOW TO CULTIVATE A HEALTHY RELATIONSHIP TO SELF

In working with our connection with our self, two main actions assist. These are:

- Exploring the current relationship to self and taking stock of the reality. In the spirit of mindfulness, noting what is present without seeking to censor, adjust, make different or manipulate in any way.
- Building the relationship with self in a healthy, straightforward and conscious way.

EXPLORING THE RELATIONSHIP TO SELF

REFLECTION POINT

Take a pause now from reading. I want you to find five words to describe yourself. How do you describe yourself? Write them down.

Now note the tone of these words: are they judgement or critical? Are they appreciative? Are they derived from within you and your own life experience, or are they things other people have labelled you as? Are they realistic or is it difficult to tell?

Use this information to begin to realistically note your current connection to self.

Negative self-relationship

If you find you feel negatively towards yourself, this may be a result of external messages you have received or from previous challenging life experiences.

No baby comes into the world bristling with self-hate.

Some people have been taught that to have positive regard towards themselves is a bad thing, and even a dangerous thing. It is associated with conceit and arrogance, 'having tickets on yourself', 'being up yourself', the tall poppy syndrome and other concerns. Feelings of shame and unworthiness can surface when you allow this to be different or challenge these kinds of thoughts.

Difficult life circumstances and experiences can also shape the way we feel towards ourselves and young people tend to often attribute much responsibility to themselves—far more than usually, realistically rests with them. This can affect the relationship to self and self-assessment.

Every person deserves to be respected and needs to feel loved and connected. What is the point or advantage of negating yourself?

The set-up of our relationship to ourselves

There is a crossover with understanding messages received about our emotions growing up, as looked at in a previous chapter. These messages—spoken directly or unspoken and received indirectly—set up many of our patterns in how we feel about ourselves as emotional beings and more broadly.

Awareness of the set-up we continue to act out is especially important to begin to recognise and review in our adult life. It can take time to recognise these filters fully because they constitute our version of 'normal'. They are the only version of reality we know until critically reviewed, but once we do, we can bring in a healthy 'critical gaze' to what we live automatically.

REFLECTION POINT

Some questions to help guide you in this enquiry include:

- Was I allowed to feel positive about myself, proud of what I did?

- Was I allowed to love and like myself?

- Was I encouraged to respect myself as well as others?

- Did I see the caregivers around me allow themselves self-care, self-respect and consideration of needs?

- Was I allowed and encouraged to do things that I felt interested in and enjoyed?

Allow yourself to reflect with honesty and respect any feelings that might come if you find that you were not encouraged to develop a caring and respectful relationship with yourself. You certainly are not alone, as many caregivers, for a whole range of reasons may not facilitate this or have their limitations. This can include caregivers not having this capacity themselves.

The good news is that as human beings we are incredibly adaptable and our brains—where we form our patterns of behaviour and the emotional and cognitive filters we see the world through—have been discovered to have great flexibility and capacity to heal and change.

We need to give ourselves permission to like and respect ourselves. It is a must in life. And as aware, alert and conscious beings we have the opportunity to do precisely that—to correct the outdated and unhealthy psychological stances we may have absorbed earlier in life.

Self-Love in Action

If not us, then who?

I have worked with many people over my years as a counsellor, group therapist and social worker, and there is a common pain-point amongst many. It is the longing to feel good about themselves and a struggle to be able to do so.

We all need to know we are worthy, valuable, matter and are acceptable. So often emotional storms involve this painful point of desperately needing to feel better and finding there is no-one there who can provide this to us in a way it can be received—from our self or from other people. To have others in our life who have faith in us, and care is wonderful and ideal, but it does not replace such a relationship with our self. It compliments and it enhances; and often there can be an absence of others who know how to do this, can do this, who understand the particular situation that you find yourself in. But *you* do …

If we cannot know our own worth and offer this when we feel emotionally challenged then really, we are left at the mercy of the stormy winds and rain, without our main resource: our self.

We are our main resource. We need to be on our own side. We need to value and validate ourselves, even when things are a struggle in life. Our relationship with our self is the foundation of managing challenges and accepting all the seasons of life we experience in the best way possible.

BUILDING THE RELATIONSHIP TO SELF

Building positive feelings

Once you have made contact with yourself in a conscious way and recognise how you feel about yourself, the next step to promoting positive change is to actively, intentionally do things that contribute to building a positive relationship with self. The aim is to increase all the characteristics of a healthy relationship: self-respect, self-appreciation, self-love, self-compassion, self-discipline, accurate self-appraisal and self-care. Other characteristics can include honesty, enjoyment of self, having fun and tackling important issues and projects in your life.

REFLECTION POINT

Take a moment now and write down five things you like about yourself. They can be qualities of yourself as a person, or achievements, or values you hold and feel strongly about. There is no right or wrong as to what can go on the list. Simply find five things that you like about you!

Okay. Now, from writing that list, notice what went on there and how easy it was to come up with those things. Notice how strong your critical voice was during that exercise.

- Did it feel okay to be positive about yourself?
- Are you allowed to have positive feelings about yourself?
- Did any other things come up as you wrote this?

The truth is that once upon a time this was difficult for me as for many of my clients that I have worked with. It can feel like owning your good stuff is something that many of us have never been encouraged to do … particularly for ourselves.

Praise can often come in ways that is very much about other people in our lives, pleasing those people and fulfilling (and exceeding) expectations of society. This exercise is just about *you* and your own opinion of yourself.

On my list today, as I wrote this part of the chapter, were:

- my creativity
- my determination to tackle challenges
- being organised
- my value of adventure
- my education and learning.

Doing these types of exercises assists in really getting to know yourself, and most importantly, dedicating time to doing so. Being able to know what you enjoy, appreciate, love, like, respect about yourself flows very readily once you bring your awareness in and spend time exploring this important question.

PRACTICE POINT: Building Positive Regard for Self

Make a list of ten activities to cultivate your relationship with self

This practice is about deliberately identifying ten things that cultivate and maintain a positive relationship with yourself.

Putting activities into everyday life that focus on nurturing and cultivating positive, respectful feelings towards yourself, is a central practice in promoting the relationship to self. These activities assist in maintaining a real and close connection with you. They serve to short-circuit and disrupt negative patterns that may be habitual. There is something about 'actions speak louder than words' that holds true.

The activities you choose for your list must be things that appeal to you. Building healthy self-regard means doing things that generate positive feelings. If things are unappealing or a chore then it is unlikely that they will become regular or serve this purpose. One of the things that can complicate selection is a barrel-load of 'shoulds'. 'Shoulds' are ideas of what you ought to be doing and these are ideas of the mind: something you have read, things other people have said to you, ideas promoted in popular culture. They are often independent of the emotional side or feeling side of self and may even represent an attempt to override and dominate the emotions.

So, a guide for choosing activities is to go with what 'pleases your heart'. It must be real—real and simple—and you are the adjudicator of this, ultimately.

Use the following list of potential self-nurturing, self-caring, self-respecting activities to kickstart exploring options for your own list and creating deliberate practices for nurturing your relationship with self.

Having a bath
Walking the dog
Hiking in nature
Swimming in the ocean, river or lake
Buying new clothes
Cooking a meal
Planning some alone time
Planning meeting friends
Gardening
Reading a good book
Attending free local events like markets, fetes, carnivals, and festivals
Putting fresh sheets on the bed
Going to a concert
Participating in a club
Trying a new interest/class
Practising meditation or yoga
Listening to a podcast
Going to a talk or lecture
Going to the beach

Going out for dinner
Planning a holiday
Going for a drive
Working out at the gym
Going to a café
Cleaning the home space
Having a massage
Relaxing, doing nothing
Keeping a day free
Volunteering to be part of something
Writing a journal
Organising an area of life/possessions
Creating music playlists
Dancing
Patting a dog or cat
Going and seeing a concert of an entertainer you really like
Going fishing
Going camping
Seeing a movie

Activities I use to maintain a positive and caring connection with myself include walking in nature for some lengthy distances at least a few times a week, cooking healthy meals, having some good reading material, staying connected with friends and family regularly, seeing live music, and being part of different festivals and yearly events.

Please note: These are simple, ordinary activities, but it is the way they are done, the quality of awareness and intention that counts. They are about fostering time to prioritise self—the opposite of being in a mad rush, with the mind busy on other things, distracted, and not noticing what you are doing.

Time to tune in with yourself

These kinds of activities are about giving yourself time to connect with and check in on yourself. It is so easy to go through the day with a focus on other people and things we need to get to. It is very easy to not think much about you.

Tuning into yourself and the practice of doing this regularly, benefits not only you but everyone around you and everything you do. It 'ups' the quality of being and doing because it increases your authenticity and presence in a meaningful way.

Developing real contact and attunement with yourself also develops skills of allowing space and feelings to be there. As previously stated, practising mindfulness—being present in the current moment and simply seeing what is, without judgement, and with acceptance—provides the foundation for tuning into self, and this is the cornerstone of cultivating a solid relationship to you.

Solidifying our sense of self

One of the consequences of frequent emotional storms, of dealing with intense emotions, can be that it keeps people in the constant business of dealing with being triggered. This takes attention and focus away from experiencing ourselves in other ways, within life.

It can result in being externally focused as a key defining force of a sense of self, looking outwards to others for reference, looking outwards for ongoing challenge and triggers with vigilance. It can interfere with developing an innate, solid sense of self that we inhabit—and update—as we move through life. We all need to be able to feel who we are as a person, to actively relate to a tangible and fully developing sense of self. Emotional storms can hijack a fuller sense of who we are as people and the experiences that facilitate development of that, narrowing our view.

Without this sense, relating and moving through life can feel stressful and insecure. Life is full of decisions and making them has consequences. If the sense of self is fragile or underdeveloped, it can be hard to know what is the best choice or what is right for you.

There are a few simple processes that assist with getting a better handle on who you are as a person.

These include:

- Trialling likes and dislikes. Experimenting or trying new things helps develop understanding of your own preferences, identifying strengths and talents, as well as areas that are more challenging. We all have our strengths and areas of challenge.
- Another helpful process is identifying values. There are a number of approaches but the aim is the same: to know the values that are most important to you as a person, and then being able to apply those more consciously in your life, to allow them to guide you in choices and staying on track. (See the free Values Identification Offer at the end of the book.)

Self-validation

Validation has been described in earlier chapters and is key in achieving an empowered relationship with our emotions. Self-validation is also significant in our relationship to ourselves.

We need to back ourselves, at times when others may not accept our truth, may openly challenge our position, may even tell us that our experience is not the way it should be, is not right.

Self-validation comes into a power of its own when we can accept that others may see things differently to us but not abandon our truth. Self-validation is, in the face of challenges and questions, when we can stand by what we perceive, and emotionally validate what simply is so to us —the *isness* of our emotional experience. It does not mean you have to act beyond confirming, affirming your inner knowing. A healthy relationship with self and your emotions requires the capacity to validate yourself independent of other people.

A well-rounded relationship

Just like any relationship, in your relationship with self, there can be days of harmony, and there can be days of conflict and disappointment. In any healthy relationship, all of these are possible. Perfection in relationships is impossible to define or achieve generally.

Sometimes we may not know what we want or what is right for us; we may choose something, experiment, and go down tracks that turn out to be disappointing. In these cases, cultivating honesty is valuable. Yes, at times, anger and regret can occur and need acknowledgment; they provide feedback about choices and valuable information for future choices. Self-forgiveness and self-compassion are wonderful companions alongside self-honesty to consciously develop for such instances.

Practising honesty *and* self-compassion are the golden double act to remaining on course with your relationship with self.

PRACTICE POINT: Self-Compassion Exercise

When you next notice yourself in circumstances where you feel emotional stress—pain, fear, anxiety, sadness, or anger—seek to regard yourself with an attitude of kindness, understanding and care (self-compassion).

- Seek to suspend criticism or judgement as much as possible.
- Seek to suspend jumping into trying to 'fix' the situation.
- When any criticism, judgement or urge to fix comes in, gently refocus on the feelings of kindness, self-understanding and compassion towards yourself. Recognise the current state of pain and difficulty.
- Gently feel all these qualities of self-compassion with every inhalation and exhalation.
- If it helps, apply to yourself the same care you would to a small child who needs comfort and reassurance.

IN SUMMARY

To consciously look at how we relate to ourselves, how we regard and treat ourselves, and the beliefs and notions we carry within, is the central focus of this key area. Feelings towards our self, set up our emotional reality, flowing into the way we show up in life. They potentially compound challenging emotions when we do not have a healthy connection with ourselves and know our worth. Alternately, a positive, healthy relationship with self provides a resource to draw on during emotional storms, and generally sets up a person for a more optimistic, straightforward trajectory in their world.

TAKEAWAY PRACTICES

- Check in with your current connection to self through words to describe you as a person, words to describe what you like or love about yourself.

- Explore the influence of the past set-up: are you allowed to feel positive about yourself? Gently reframe negative ideas with the fact that to have a healthy relationship and connection with yourself is important.

- Explore yourself through identifying your values.

- Write a list of activities that cultivate your connection with yourself and provide time to build your relationship to self.

- Practise the **Self-Compassion Exercise.**

CHAPTER 9

Relationship with Others

Our connection with others represents a primary part of life, determining much about how we feel. Emotions are like the 'superhighway' of relating and a pathway to forming, shaping and assessing our relationships. Emotions are central in close or significant connection with others, and therefore this is an important area for building better understanding, navigation skills and appreciation of our emotional selves, as they come into play through our connections.

Relationships with other people is a key area where feelings arise. They are triggered during interactions with others, through concerns, tensions or issues arising within a relationship. Equally, within relationships emotions arise naturally during developments in intimacy, care, sharing of experiences, playfulness and fun, that are usually strongly desired.

WHY DO PEOPLE MATTER?

Other human beings matter in direct connection to our fight-or-flight system and the question of our survival. Our earliest life experiences are based on a total dependency on others, unlike many other types of animal young. As babies, humans are vulnerable and helpless. They require care from other people for survival; we need others and others must take care of us.

During this time, as we develop, other people who care for us provide several critical things related to our emotional selves:
- direction to us around our emotions (how they are responded to and how we are educated to manage them)
- a sense of safety and security (are we reassured, are we provided with what we need, are we taken seriously and sincerely?).

In an ideal world we learn about regulating our emotions and managing them from our caregivers. This is achieved through caregivers directing us with words as well as nonverbal communications. However, it is also achieved through 'modelling'—demonstrating how they deal with their own emotions and feelings as they arise—that as youngsters we watch, observe, learn from and mimic. This becomes our version of 'normal'.

The original circumstances that we are raised in, the capacity of caregivers to be present and attend to our needs, and attend to their own needs emotionally, has a defining and shaping influence on how we then approach relationship with others throughout our life.

THE MANY TYPES OF RELATIONSHIPS

All types of relationships that populate our lives and psyche, past and present, can be related to the material within this chapter. This includes:

Family relationships

- partners
- children
- parents
- siblings
- grandparents
- grandchildren
- aunts and uncles
- cousins
- step and blended family members.

Outside of family relationships

- friends
- work colleagues
- neighbours
- associates
- people we interact with in shops and services
- community members.

People in general, in all roles in our life and through all types of encounters, can stir emotions. Because people matter, all people—known or unknown—provide a primary site of provocation of feelings within us.

Please note: The way we choose to label a relationship is ultimately up to us and language is open to meaning and reinterpretation. Such subjective meaning arises around the word *family*, that for many people includes others who are not related genetically yet have a primary closeness and significance; people 'feel like family' or fulfil our idea of family beyond traditional definitions.

ABSENCE OF RELATING AND RELATIONSHIPS

For some people, avoidance of people—an absence of relationships and retreat from the world of people—has been a way of managing challenging emotions stirred up through connection. For others, the absence of people, particularly family, through circumstances such as death, adoption or being fostered, due to unreliable or hurtful connections resulting in distancing and estrangement, can mean that the emotions you have around relating are focused on an absence or loss. This is still a version of the emotional impacts of relating—it is the other side of the same coin of connection. It involves the very relationships and connections that we carry within our hearts, even without contact.

The world is full of people and by the very way human beings are designed, others matter. This chapter is for everyone whether you are surrounded by others or feel the absence of them, by choice or not.

REFLECTION POINT

Do I manage my emotions by avoiding, or minimising relating? Do I escape from relating because it raises intense emotions?

What kind of connections are present in my life that I count as significant? Do I have 'family' that are not blood connections?

EXPECT THE UNEXPECTED

The feelings that arise towards other people are spontaneous responses or reactions to what we encounter.

So often feelings for other people can develop independent of rational thinking and logic, taking us by surprise, changing unexpectedly and holding a strong bearing on the course of the relationship.

We do not have control ultimately over anyone but ourselves. Other people can be unpredictable and increase the sense of things being beyond our control with how we may be emotionally impacted. This element of relationship is therefore poignant and potentially a key triggering factor of feelings.

BENEFITS OF REFLECTING ON RELATING WITH OTHERS

The benefits of bringing awareness to the emotional dimensions within relationships include the following:

We are social animals

Emotional bonds with others are one of the most important and significant parts of life: they matter. As human beings we are tribal and social creatures that seek connection and to live in groups. Frequently, family provides this immediate group context in some shape or form. There is a kind of inbuilt longing to belong, and implicit in this is connection and bonding. This taps into the fight-or-flight aspect of emotions, as discussed in previous chapters. Belonging and acceptance—being valued and able to be yourself within relationships—translates into security and safety. Within a group there is a pooling of resources and support, all essential to survival.

Emotions allow connection

Relationships are about connection and links between two people. Emotions are part of the primary substance that bonds us with another in significant, key relationships. Emotions provide feedback about how we feel in the relationship and tend to be a defining key of the significance and importance of it to us.

Builds self-understanding

Understanding how you operate within relationships, and the patterns of behaviour that connecting with others brings out, all facilitates a better understanding of how we cope and operate in a social world. It helps facilitate a stronger relationship with self, which then builds self-understanding and skills for cultivating increasingly satisfying connection with others. It helps to better understand impacts of past relating experiences and with awareness, heal wounds and correct old patterns.

A NOTE FOR THE BEREAVED AND RELATIONSHIPS WITH PEOPLE WHO HAVE PASSED AWAY

Relationships live on after the loved one has walked this earth. They live within us and often remain a tangible part of our relationship circle. The loss in itself, the grief, can be a key part of what is felt when the deceased person is remembered. For other people, acceptance may be there of the passing, they have come to terms with the loss and their grief process, and other aspects of the relationship live on as the main focus.

Researchers and authors Phyllis Silverman, Steven Nickman and Dennis Kless introduced the phrase 'continuing bonds' as an important concept in their revolutionary view on grief and bereavement.

KEY CONCEPT: Continuing Bonds

This phrase was designed to capture the way in which a relationship with someone remains living and significant beyond a person's life, that for those still living, the bond with that person can continue on in a real, legitimate form. The impact of someone who may not be living can remain deeply significant and felt; it can account for current emotions in many common ways.

These can include difficult emotions such as:
- missing and yearning for the loved one
- anger at the person for going
- loneliness
- feeling abandoned
- grief for what is lost
- loss of belonging and connection.

However, it can also offer emotional experiences that are desired, give sustenance and positive effects, such as:

- feeling connected
- feeling ongoing love
- feeling safe and secure
- feeling emotionally supported
- feeling connection and belonging
- feeling understood.

These feelings can often be minimised or dismissed because the message given by the living can be that the person is now gone, they are no longer there and therefore any feelings about them are not real or valid. For many people loss is confronting and difficult to deal with, so their responses can reflect that.

REFLECTION POINT

Do I feel connection with loved ones that have died? Do I allow feeling an ongoing relationship with them? Am I affected by people around me who may judge my connection?

Take note of any relationships that emotionally serve and support you with a loved one who has passed away. Allow yourself to validate this relationship for what it offers you today.

Note any judgements or dismissive statements from other people and allow differences to simply be there. Choose who you may speak to about your own continuing bonds, if anyone.

RELATIONSHIPS WITH PETS

I would be an extraordinarily rich woman if I had a dollar for every time a client told me that one of the most important relationships in their life was with their pet, a dog or cat. And then they apologise ... Or say something with the word *silly* included. The message they give me, and what they feel, is that in some way that relationship with their pet is less than or should not matter as much as it does.

But the truth is it does matter and is significant to them without doubt. And for that reason, I want to underline the validity and importance of these kind of relationships in people's lives.

In a recent Australian Broadcasting Commission survey—the Australia Talks National Survey— open to all the public, people were asked about all kind of things in their lives including pets. The findings came up with the statistic that one in three of the people surveyed stated that they preferred their pets to other people. I have had people tell me that their reason for living was the love for their pet.

Pets are significant because:
- they are always around and tend to be with people in their home
- they do not speak, or use words for complex interactions
- they tend to be loyal
- they demonstrate care and positive feelings towards their master
- they provide opportunity for physical affection and touch.

THE SIGNIFICANCE OF PAST RELATIONSHIPS

In working with people in therapy and counselling, in therapy groups and brief assessments, relationships past and present are common key factors in people's presenting distress, grief, concern, fear, anger, jealousy, hurt, love, happiness, support and comfort.

Part of the reality of relating is that all of one person's history meets all of another person's history, as we each may carry it. And how we manage to carry our own past determines how we naturally bring it into our current relationships and encounters with people. We may have certain areas of our history—impacts of life experience—that are sensitive and continue to shape us in the present day. The potential for those things to be carried into current relating is high and commonplace.

TOOLS FOR APPROACHING RELATING AND EMOTIONAL HEALTH: ATTACHMENT THEORY

In understanding ourselves and emotions within relationships, there is an important theory that provides significant insight. It is called Attachment Theory and focuses on the importance of emotional development centred in relationship.

KEY CONCEPT: Attachment

Attachment refers to the emotional bond that forms between people. It occurs at all stages of life, within relationships, but is particularly significant between an infant and their primary caregivers, or significant others when dependent.

Attachment Theory first focused on the development of attachment for children, but it now extends to understanding adult relating styles carried through from early life experiences. It particularly examines how an individual copes with stress, perceived threats, or separation within a relationship. It highlights the capacity for trust and security.

A famous research procedure called the Strange Situation was devised by Mary Ainsworth in the 1960s in America, and used for research on attachment into the 1970s. The procedure or protocol observed pairs of infants (aged between 12–24 months) and parents. The study had a rigid structure which involved the leaving and returning of the parent and a stranger. The behaviour of the infant belied security, emotion management and the kind of attachment developed towards the parent: how did the infant interact with the parent, how did they react to the parent leaving, how did they react to a stranger entering the room, how did the infant react to the return of the parent?

In Ainsworth's original experiment of the Strange Situation she identified three different styles of attachment in the infants to their caregiver from observation. They are as follows:

Secure attachment: when children behaved in a way that showed they felt they could rely on their caregivers for needs of protection, proximity or closeness and emotional support. The infants were observed to feel safe to leave the caregiver and explore the wider unfamiliar environment, relying on the caregiver to reliably be there to return to. They tolerated the parent leaving and the presence of the stranger.

Anxious-ambivalent attachment: when the infant felt anxiety in an unfamiliar environment and with separation from the caregiver but equally did not feel secure when the caregiver returned. They did not explore the unfamiliar environment and were often observed clinging to the parent.

Avoidant attachment: when the infant avoided the caregiver generally, did not explore the unfamiliar environment and did not show much response to the parent being present, leaving, returning or to the presence of a stranger.

Later, a fourth style of attachment was named.
Disorganised attachment: when the infant displayed no attachment to the caregiver and experienced significant disorder within due to the exceedingly difficult situation this raises for them in the relationship. Changes to the environment including the people

present provoked reactions without consistent patterns, often with distress in the infant.

Attachment can be extremely valuable in highlighting our expectations of others through the flow on of early caregiver experiences, which then goes on to continue to function in adult relationships. Once we identify our own style we can then bring consciousness to shifting thinking and behaviour, challenging the basis for painful feelings, and increasing awareness of when attachment concerns get touched.

The good news is that old wounds can be healed in current, healthy, corrective relationships. Our capacity to shift established psychological patterns is increasingly recognised and includes what is termed the 'plasticity' of our brains—our current and future life experiences and relationships with others can shape and rewire impacts from the past. The professional relationship with a therapist (counsellor, psychologist, psychiatrist, social worker, youth worker) is one such relationship where secure attachment can be experienced. This was explored in Michael Wallin's book *Attachment in Psychotherapy*.

Due to the traumatic nature of insecure attachment styles, working with a professional is advised if you recognise emotional challenges flowing from your early attachment experiences, that you want to explore more fully.

RELATIONSHIPS AS A MIRROR

When we connect with another person and allow ourselves to feel that connection, to take that connection in, then it inevitably stirs things within ourselves that we can notice, if we pay attention. Interaction with another person will naturally stir a response that often includes emotions of varying kinds and intensity. The kind of interactions where this may not occur so much are often where the connection is not so significant or valued by us. It could be everyday business-like dealings with retail workers or the postman or the person at the drive-thru window.

Or it also could be family relations and associates where you have resolved that it is not so emotionally important to you.

However, all interactions with other people are potentially emotionally triggering or stirring. As seen in the chapter around the messages received from the external world, through personal family connections and experiences, and also through society, culture and religion as whole, emotional positions, wounds and attitudes can be set up. It is usually in the meeting with others that this past history of experience can get triggered.

Relationships are a mirror in that through relating with another, we see ourselves. We can see things about ourselves deeply connected with feeling when opening up to another and allowing vulnerability.

I had a client who had been brought up in a family that was very authoritarian. She was always being told what she could and couldn't do and was frequently shamed. Her way of emotionally surviving in this environment was to try to attend to other people's demands of her as best she could, in the hope of getting approval and keeping the peace.

As she got older this tendency to aim for doing what others approved of and not rocking the boat infiltrated all her relationships to varying degrees. It had become her prime default mode in relating—emotionally driven, centred on seeking care and approval, never creating tension or conflict, and striving for harmony at all costs. At the same time, within relationships, because of always deferring to others to determine her own behaviour, she experienced growing feelings of 'never being seen'. The client came to a position of feeling anger at never feeling seen. When she came for counselling, she brought a situation that she recognised didn't make sense but kept happening, as an example of this.

When this woman went to cross a road and was at a corner, she naturally checked for passing cars. Whenever a car approached the corner and then turned without using its indicator while she was standing there, she felt incredible anger—that the driver was not acknowledging her, not seeing her, and dismissing her by not communicating that they were turning. This woman would feel furious and upset inside at not being seen. She was acutely aware that this did not make sense, but nevertheless these feelings kept getting provoked, independent of her logical mind.

This client's situation gives a great example of how connection with others, even a random person driving by, can trigger us emotionally. The capacity for total strangers to elicit feelings can be for some people as significant as with people where there is a relationship.

We can project feelings onto all situations if there is a wound or vulnerability—a sensitivity—sitting there within, in relation to others. Relating as a mirror was live and active in this woman's experience.

By paying attention to it and bringing in awareness of what was happening, within counselling, the client was able to appreciate how much being seen by others mattered to her. She also saw that she needed to begin to learn how to show herself more in relating, versus her default of allowing others to lead and dominate.

PRACTICE POINT: Look in the Mirror

When around other people, using the practice of mindful awareness in the moment, note inner reactions and responses to the people you spend time around. Take time after connecting with others to review what may get touched in you, including any emotional content. Tune into the other as a mirror that shows you things about yourself (as opposed to about themselves).

Note how easy or difficult this practice is and experiment with this as a means to enhance relationship skills and understanding in your different relationships.

EXPECTATION OF OTHERS

We all bring expectations into a relationship—the things that we presume are going to be present, are reasonable to ask for, and automatically relied upon. Expectations can reflect our own values and the way we want to be treated; they represent our standards for relationships and exert a healthy influence over how we are in relating.

However, expectations can also be things that represent our own inner relationship programming and not something universally understood or reasonable to expect. These automatic expectations can then cause tension, conflict and misunderstanding between people. Some common expectations that can be brought to a relationship include the following:

- seeking approval
- seeking reassurance
- needing recognition and validation
- not tolerating different views to your own
- wanting the other to agree with you all the time
- wanting the other person to know what you are thinking/feeling without having to say.

When these types of expectations get out of hand is when the things that are naturally desired in a close relationship can tip into stresses and excessive demands.

REFLECTION POINT

Reflect on any patterns of expectations that you bring to your relationships. Try not to judge, defend or feel 'wrong or right' about what you notice. Simply note any tendencies that you may have and reflect on how they serve you in your relating.

COMMUNICATION AND LISTENING

Our capacity to communicate, to express ourselves to another, together with the other person's own communication capacity, can determine much within a relationship and the emotions present for both. In relating, what is within our control includes how we communicate and express ourselves, that gives us the best chance of facilitating the kind of relationship that we hope for and showing who we are as a person. Therefore, developing our own communication skills is a valuable endeavour. Effective communication and expression skills can be learned by anyone.

When studying counselling, a foundation of training is called 'microskills'—specific learned skills to be present and communicate with a client. They are simple things—deceptively simple—yet have powerful effects on the quality of communication and rapport with another person.

While in my counselling training, a number of us trainees noted how these microskills naturally began to slip into our communication with others—in social situations and personal relationships. Why? Because they were lovely, respectful, easy-to-do things, that enhanced communication and connection with others. And not only that, we all noted that indeed these simple things really encouraged others to feel good in our company.

Some of these microskills include attending behaviour to the other person through body language, orientation or position of your body, eye contact and facial expression (nonverbal communication as noted previously); as well as ways of noting and reflecting back what the other person is expressing; and ways of questioning and focusing.

One of these basic microskills is called 'active listening' and it is offered here as a taster of communication skills.

Listening is a powerful act. It is not an act that gives power away nor holds power over another: it is an act of respect and presumed equality in the communication. To actively listen and allow the other to say what they say does not at all mean you are agreeing with or even condoning their thoughts. You are listening and really hearing another with full attention. Active listening means being present, open and focused on the other person as they speak.

PRACTICE POINT: Active Listening
Active listening means:
- being present
- fully listening to the other with all your senses
- paying attention to the other as the focus.

Allow inner and outer distractions to come and go in the background if possible. Resist focusing on your own thoughts such as what you want to say or how you want to reply when your turn to speak comes.

Please note: You will certainly notice if the other person does not give you space to also speak, or is not present to you equally; that is simply good information to have about the other and your relationship.

Active listening requires security in yourself. As someone who was often flooded with overwhelm around others, I had many times where I was silent and felt overrun by another talking *at* me. This was not a pleasant experience, it can be traumatic for many people, and is definitely not what is being described here.

If I notice someone wants to talk *at* me, is not paying attention to me at all, is venting or downloading, and not giving space to respond, I take note. I may choose to persevere in relating to see if this changes as the person gets things out, but if it doesn't, I find a way to respectfully move on.

UNDERSTANDING AUTHENTIC ASSERTIVENESS
Another helpful concept to consider in how you interact with others relates to the oft-misunderstood concept of being assertive. The traditional spectrum of behaviour included in this concept is represented in the following diagram:

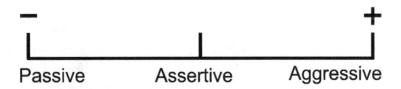

Passive   Assertive   Aggressive

The Assertiveness Scale

Assertiveness represents a middle zone in the sliding scale of possibility. Passivity describes being without any self-agency, receiving what is without any response or reaction to what is coming towards us. Often this can be through fear, seeking of approval, a lack of sense of self or many other reasons, including combinations of these.

Aggression is marked by behaviour that seeks to overpower, strongly influence and exert oneself on another with force. This can also be driven by fear as well as a desire to be in control, a lack of tolerance and anger. Aggression can feel threatening and the person on the receiving end of it usually detects a high level of emotion.

Assertiveness can often be confused with aggression, yet it is something markedly different.

Assertiveness is described as behaviour and attitude that respects yourself *while* respecting the other.

It is a beautiful concept; including that respect for both parties is seen as possible and necessary. A key to reaching genuine assertiveness is that you are able to validate your own position, even in the face of challenge or differences of opinion. You validate the other by showing understanding of their position even if you hold a different view and do not agree.

REFLECTION POINT

Reflect on any baseline stance you may take with others along the assertiveness scale. Do you tend to sit at one point habitually and how does that serve you in your relationships?

Look for moments in life where you might be prompted to be assertive. This means respecting yourself while you also respect others in your communication and behaviour. Look for easy, non-critical points in your life where you can do this rather than bringing practice to difficult, complex and critical issues, at first. Note how this feels for you.

A FINAL WORD

This chapter on the key area of relationships with others offers a highly selective, basic summary of some concepts useful in assisting with increased understanding, navigating and valuing of emotions within relating. Relating is a vast topic and there is a huge amount of reading and books on different aspects of it, together with taking into account your own particular circumstances and patterns within connection. This chapter also goes together with the previous chapter on your relationship with self, as they are intricately linked.

IN SUMMARY

By bringing our focus to our relationships with other people, as an important area of learning about our emotions and emotional selves, we tap into an area rich with potential for building understanding, skills for better navigating emotions and also for harvesting the opportunities that these connections offer. The quality of relationships with others, relationships and relating of all types, is a flow-on effect from the relationship and feelings towards yourself, together with other factors such as the way others around you relate and manage their own emotional self.

TAKEAWAY PRACTICES

- Note the relationships in your life. Include family and friends, associates and other community connections. Include connections with people who have died that you feel a continuing bond with. Include pets. Draw a map of these connections with yourself as the centre point.

- Practise **Active Listening** when next engaged in conversation with someone. Notice how it may change the experience and connection with the other.

- Notice when you may be passive, assertive or aggressive in your interactions with others. Experiment with consciously choosing where you sit along this scale and notice the feelings that this generates in yourself and others.

- Observe yourself mindfully in your relationships, including awareness around expectations, impacts of past experiences, recognising attachment styles and the relationship as a mirror. Observe to build your self-understanding and awareness of any automatic modes of relating.

CHAPTER 10

Harvesting the Riches

E motions provide much richness and texture within our lives that can easily be taken for granted. More than that, with the intense emotions associated with the fight-or-flight system and our negativity bias—of loss, fear, impacts of abuse or trauma, of heartbreak and struggle—emotions can feel like a problem to be solved.

However, beyond the 'good versus bad' judgements around emotions, avoiding condemnation of challenging emotions that are a valid part of living life—of participating in and taking on the natural risk of participation—there are a whole host of emotions we experience when we feel safe, well, secure, loved, respected, and are flourishing, managing challenges and fulfilling our natural potential.

Throughout the recorded history of mankind—from the fields of the arts, religion and spirituality, philosophy, the humanities and social service areas to contemporary business, leadership theory, politics and history—rising beyond the level of mere survival, to excelling and fulfilling potential, has been a major theme.

Emotions are key to this: they offer the unique stuff of life that cannot be compared with anything else.

The benefits of our emotional experiences in life have been touched upon throughout the book and in this chapter, the focus is on harvesting the riches so we can:

- recognise the psychology of emotional wellness and understand emotional needs for wellbeing
- learn how to access and build emotional wellness and wellbeing in life, no matter what may be happening.

BEYOND THE PROBLEM

There is a common theme that I have encountered in my counselling work with clients who are struggling with strong emotions: they can feel defeated, hopeless, lacking in power and fixated on the thing they want to be different. They can be narrowly focused on the problems at hand, which are identified by them as their source of difficult feelings. When asked about the rest of life there can be a resistance to taking attention away from what concerns them. This is understandable, as when alarmed, when feeling in danger, when the fight-or-flight mechanism is activated, attention and focus narrows upon the point of hurt and risk.

Yet the truth is, there are usually other things present in their lives or that there is the potential for. Their view of themselves and life has become very narrow.

Naturally, the concern is on the worry, but often the solution has nothing to do with the problem; the resolution can be recovering a broader gaze beyond immediate difficulties.

With this key area, the focus is upon consciously bringing in the feelings that promote wellbeing and positive regard towards yourself, the world and life. These feelings can be about already existing sources such as people and things present in life, or memories and experiences that can be recalled. These feelings can result from being opportunistic about what comes our way and the meaning we find in things.

A second part of this pins on the concept of cultivating an internal locus of control—a sense of control that is born from within rather than feeling at the mercy of external factors. This taps into the question of self-agency and generating our own trajectory of meaning and purpose independent (or in spite of) challenging conditions.

KEY CONCEPT: Locus of Control

This concept, first defined by American psychologist Julian Rotter in 1954, refers to how people may tend to attribute events and outcomes in their life. Do they see external factors beyond their own person as the reason for success or failure? Do they attribute outcomes and results in their life as due to internal factors about themselves? Where do they tend to locate the control and power over their lives?

An **internal locus** of control sees the person view themselves as controlling much of what occurs in their life. For example, with a sporting competition they see themselves as in control through their own training, preparation, ability to work in a team and athletic ability.

An **external locus** of control sees the person tend to view factors beyond themselves as the controlling factor over what happens—other people, the environment, circumstances. For example, with a sporting competition they may see the referee, weather conditions, other team members and the opposition as being in control and responsible for the results.

When we focus in on the control that we actually hold within situations the feelings about it can alter dramatically (as well as our effectiveness to manage). A storm is something that we do not have control over, however our control lies in how we respond (or react) and how we are able to hold ourselves. It lies in how we may resource ourselves to meet the challenge.

REFLECTION POINT

Utilise the concept of internal versus external loci of control. Notice as you go through your day if you have a default locus of control. How do you tend to see your own level of self-agency and control in your life? Do you tend to feel circumstances beyond your control exert much influence over you? Do you recognise your own responsibility and opportunities to take charge?

MASLOW'S HEIRARCHY OF NEEDS

Albert Maslow first outlined his famous Hierarchy of Needs in 1943. This remains a very pertinent lens through which to view emotional wellness in relation to needs. It is often these very needs that are keenly linked with our emotional state, and are at the heart of emotional storms we may experience as we move through life. Survival has a strong emotional edge whether it entails facing a perceived threat or through our negativity bias at play.

Maslow's psychological theory was embedded in seeking to understand what motivates people and creates emotional health. He was one of the pioneers of what would come to be called Positive Psychology—a focus away from psychological problems to focusing on what creates psychological wellbeing. Emotional health and wellness lie at the heart of psychological health. The use of the word *positive* in this key area reflects the emotions as understood through the Positive Psychology movement—emotions associated with a sense of wellbeing, aliveness and growth beyond survival.

Survival forms the essential motivation hardwired into human beings at the most basic level. Maslow's proposed hierarchy stated that the lower needs on his pyramid formed a foundation and needed to be fulfilled before a person could rise higher, working on the higher needs leading to self-actualisation. He called these higher needs 'growth needs' versus the lower 'deficiency needs', basic to survival. His model sought to raise understanding beyond mere survival into thriving.

Below is an outline of Maslow's model:

LEVEL 5 Self-actualisation needs the desire to become the most that one can be
LEVEL 4 Esteem needs respect, self-esteem, status, recognition, strength, freedom
LEVEL 3 Love and belonging needs friendship, intimacy, family, sense of connection and belonging
LEVEL 2 Safety needs personal safety, employment or financial security, resources, health
LEVEL 1 Physiological needs water, air, sleep, clothing, shelter, food, reproduction

Emotional stress can be triggered at many points in Maslow's hierarchy, depending upon individual and personal history. A sense of risk or concern will evoke certain emotions of fear, anger, sadness, anxiety and all their cousins, and this can occur around physical needs all the way through to the uppermost identified need of self-actualisation.

One of the criticisms of the theory is that it is too rigid and fixed, but Maslow did indicate that the order of needs being fulfilled was flexible. When I worked in the homelessness sector, staff noted that people who struggled to secure housing did not necessarily remain at this basic level of the pyramid. There were examples of people achieving higher order needs, despite being homeless. Yes, the struggle was more substantial without the most basic of resources in place, yet it happened on a daily level. People worked on their relationship with self before having a sense of belonging; people without housing appeared to have rich creative, intellectual and spiritual lives.

The Hierarchy of Needs offers a solid springboard for bringing awareness to a broad range of our needs and the emotional content of these in motion in our lives.

REFLECTION POINT

Reflect on the different levels of need and motivation as set out by Maslow's Hierarchy of Needs. Check in on how you would assess meeting your own needs according to each level of his hierarchy.

Note areas of fulfilment and areas where you feel a gap in needs being met. Observe and build awareness of your circumstances and the impacts this may have through emotional stress or alternatively, emotional security and wellbeing.

THE PALACE IS RELATIVE

Having spent many years travelling and living in India, my perspective on home, safety, abundance and what makes me happy has shifted substantially. Growing up in a Western democratic country with numerous opportunities for a safe, secure life, I took for granted much before I set off to experience a third world, developing country. While the levels of material comfort and security were profoundly different in India, the rich cultural, spiritual and collective character of the country showed me a very different depth of richness.

The challenges of that first time travelling were many and intense. I was twenty-three years old and I ventured off alone to the Indian subcontinent for my first adult trip overseas. During this time (as many people know about travel) the unexpected happens and what is meant to be a 'holiday' can turn into various kinds of nightmares and endurance tests. John Lennon wasn't kidding when he said, 'Life happens while you're busy making other plans'. That is real when travelling!

The culture shock was profound, being immersed in ways and expectations of people and life that were different to anything I had experienced. Travelling solo left me vulnerable at times to feeling lonely, annoyed, fearful and angry.

When travelling alone there is no buffer of a companion to assist with management and the processing of experiences and emotions. At times I wanted to come home but persevered, buoyed by experiences of adventure, wonder, happiness, connection with fellow strangers also travelling, as well as striving to keep the commitment I had made to travel for a certain amount of time. I learnt about the various cultural ways and absorbed the lessons around appreciation of difference. I found common threads of humanity, pleasure in the arts of this country and through it all, learnt much about myself as a person.

When I returned home after six months of this travel through India, I was somehow seasoned, changed, tired yet triumphant. I had stayed the course despite enormous challenges emotionally, for all the above reasons. The commitment to stay the course, to follow through, to be open and expand my horizons had been a mixed bag of experiences. It certainly was not for everyone, but for me it had tested me in ways I could not have fathomed before leaving.

I recall my first night home. I was sleeping in a makeshift bed on the floor. My mother was in a nearby room, having come to greet me on my arrival back from my journey. I was in a small apartment in a suburb of Sydney, sleeping on the floor and in that moment, I thought to myself, 'If this is all I ever have, I am indeed a rich woman'.

I was aware of the material modesty but coming from a third world country where people carved out meaningful, happy existences with very little, where the shift moved away from the material, where things were valued and appreciated because they weren't taken for granted, where the focus shifted to the immediate and enough was enough if it meant you had food and shelter and connection, I felt so secure and emotionally well. I was rich with an inner sense of safety and satisfaction, after an arduous journey that had pushed me beyond my limits.

This feeling has never left me, despite times of emotional challenge. At times I catch myself, often when I lie in bed, with clean sheets, and a roof over my head, a space to rest safely, with a locked door, electricity and running water, acknowledging 'my palace' and I feel immensely rich. It is to some degree about safety and security, but beyond that it is about emotional wellness and riches. This feeling from almost thirty years ago endures. To a great extent the palace is with me wherever I may go because I carry it within.

The feeling of richness beyond material means, or when enough is enough, remains. This kind of experience taps into a pivotal concept and practice to take stock of what you assess as the 'good' in your life.

PRACTICE POINT: Find Three Things

American psychologist Martin Seligman, a leading force in the positive psychology field, recognised and researched the power of regularly reflecting on three things that had gone well each day as a regular practice. By consciously focusing on this and writing it down, it was found to have beneficial effects on emotional wellbeing with long-lasting effects for many.

Instructions for Find Three Things
- Each night make time to write down three things from the current day that went well.
- Write down why you think they went well.
- Do this practice over a week or more to train your attention and focus on positive things happening in your life, small or big.

PRACTICE POINT: Gratitude Journal

Another popular activity that is in the same direction as Find Three Things is to write a journal regularly of what you are grateful for. Writing this regularly helps to remind yourself of the things in your life that are associated with feelings of wellbeing. It can be used for ongoing practice as well as reading back on during times of emotional difficulty or vulnerability.

GRATITUDE, WELLBEING AND MEMORIES

Memories and past experiences offer a means to tap into all kinds of feelings and emotions. In accordance with the fight-or-flight system and the negativity bias, zooming into potential risks to head them off can be a default setting in our psychology; we can also automatically zoom into memories that align with this, as part of this protective mechanism. Equally though, broadening what is accessed from the memory bank can assist with achieving emotional balance and generating wellbeing feelings. Shifting the internal gaze consciously in this way also tends to cultivate a more realistic and balanced perspective.

For many years I mourned the loss of my father and to this day, it sometimes returns. He died when I was fourteen years old, diagnosed with pancreatic and colon cancer at age forty-nine, dying nine months later. The pain felt was of the loss as well as the disruption to a 'normal' teenage life onwards, and a sense of tragedy and injustice. My family was permanently changed.

For many years, the association with my father was around his demise—the way he died, the suddenness, the funeral, the lonely struggle afterwards when I returned to boarding school, the shock. In my early thirties, during one of my many stints in therapy, I named in passing the loss of my father and how I felt about it. It tapped me into awful feelings of loss, longing and the time during his illness and hospitalisation.

The therapist I was seeing at this time listened and then simply asked, 'I like the sound of your father, tell me what he was like?' That simple question opened a doorway into a room within, that I had not entered for a very long time. I had forgotten that that room, those many rooms, full of the life I had shared with my father, the memories and experiences growing up, existed. The sadness, shock, and pain of losing him had eclipsed all else. However, there was so much more that existed, was real and significant, that mattered, beyond his death. It was the very stuff that I was mourning the loss of.

During the rest of that therapy session I spoke about my father and memories of when he was just my father, not sick or the centre of a tragedy—just simply my father. I was encouraged to remember again, and it brought back feelings of wellbeing, safety, security, fun, guidance, adventure and appreciation, that I had not accessed for an exceptionally long time. In one hour of speaking, I recovered many years of good feeling, of love and connection with my father, a feeling of peace and quiet acceptance. I discovered that day in therapy that it was all still there within, available to me. In that one hour I experienced the potency of memories and the way memories can be forgotten and recalled. I also tapped into the power of memory to assist with restoring emotional wellness.

The human mind is indeed a miraculous thing.

REFLECTION POINT

I want you to think of three memories or experiences, recent or long ago, that evoke emotions within of wellbeing. They do not have to be significant events; meaning is a personal thing, no matter what anyone else may tell you. Take the time now to recall three memories that please your heart.

Notice what happened when you recall these emotionally. Jot down what you notice, identifying the feelings that arise and the impact it has on you.

These heartening moments from the past—memories, significant words spoken to you, acknowledgment, recognition or an achievement— are all carried within you and accessible at any moment. Although those times and circumstances may be over now, recalling these, reminding yourself, can provide ongoing emotional sustenance in the present moment.

BANKING FEELINGS OF WELLBEING

Emotions that enhance wellbeing often have a few different effects. They can energise you and make you feel alive, they can facilitate a sense of peace, they can bring satisfaction and pride, they can bring a sense of love and connection, admiration, longing or respect. For many people wellbeing can take different forms depending on past experiences and current challenges.

When we have an unexpected expense come up our reaction to this, the level of stress this may cause or not, often depends on how much money we already have sitting in the bank account. Have we made enough deposits to cover the withdrawal needed now? Equally, when challenging emotions crop up the impact that they have on us also depends on how we are travelling emotionally already and how much challenge and emotional stress we have had recently. How do our emotional deposits compare to what we need to make an emotional withdrawal?

We need to make deposits of good feeling (or feeling good) into our emotional bank accounts whenever we have the opportunity. And we need to make regular opportunities to do so.

The benefits of banking positive emotions include:
- builds resilience for times when you feel challenged
- builds self-understanding and a sense of control
- can provide us with a go-to self-care tool bag
- taps into our own self-agency around our emotions (self-regulation, self-management)
- can provide a sense of competence in times when other factors may test our feelings of competency.

REFLECTION POINT

Write down five things in your life that assist you in banking meaningful emotions, feel-good things that are grounded and you recognise as healthy (or neutral or positive on the consequences scale from Chapter 7). These can be things that you know you can turn to, to gain a sense of pleasure, safety, soothing, joy, peace, connection, belonging, excitement, aliveness, relaxation or anything else that enhances your sense of emotional wellbeing. One of the measures that I personally use is to ask myself, 'Does this give me energy and revitalise me?' I am looking for these kinds of effects.

Today my list went like this:
- walking in nature
- trying a new restaurant
- doing nothing, sitting on my couch
- going for a drive
- creating a new music playlist with a theme.

Below are some suggested activities that may resonate with you:

- Calling a friend for a talk
- Arranging a catch-up meeting (coffee, lunch or dinner)
- Walking in nature
- Sitting in a tranquil spot
- Taking a day off
- Planning and taking a holiday
- Writing a bucket list
- Writing a gratitude journal
- Marking a significant occasion or anniversary
- Running
- Walking
- Swimming
- Planning a day out
- Patting your pet or grooming them
- Driving
- Getting in touch with people you care about

- Taking a ferry trip
- Visiting a museum or art gallery
- Keeping a promise
- Dancing
- Being creative (painting, sculpting, knitting, etc.)
- Participating in a community group
- Exercising and moving your body
- Watching a favourite movie
- Having a massage
- Window shopping
- Studying and learning.

PRACTICE POINT: Create a list of activities to schedule into your routine

Identify at least ten activities that you recognise as contributing to feelings of emotional wellbeing. Some may be things that are part of your daily routine and very accessible; others may be less frequent or available and require planning to get to.

Write down a list now and keep adding to it as you get inspiration and new ideas.

Consider how these will be used in your life and drawn upon to maintain effective self-care. Put this into practice for a week and review the helpfulness of this.

THE ECSTASY OF BEING PRESENT

No matter what occurs in life the capacity to be present, to stay the course, to literally be able to declare 'I did the best I can' and to know that to be true, is significant. Mindfulness, as used heavily throughout this book, offers a practice that builds the capacity to be present in life with emotions, to rise to challenges, to build resilience and assert yourself in an authentic way.

A final mindfulness practice is offered that gently invites wellbeing ...

PRACTICE POINT: Half Smile Meditation

- Sit comfortably. Allow the eyes to be closed or gently open with a softened gaze.
- Relax facial muscles and the jaw consciously.
- Allow the corners of your mouth to turn up slightly as if smiling. From the outside another person might not notice this smile as it is a subtle, slight turning up of the corners of the mouth into a 'half smile'.
- Sit, half-smiling for ten minutes or more. Notice the inner, feeling effect on you and your mood. Allow the half-smile to impact your emotional self.
- Try this as a regular practice, first thing in the morning while still lying in bed, or at times when challenging feelings may be present to gently counter them.

IN SUMMARY

The richness of all emotions, across the spectrum from desirable to undesirable, is immeasurable. The value of weathering a storm and coming out the other side cannot be denied and is a natural, healthy cycle. Equally, knowing to harvest the emotions associated with emotional wellbeing—peace, love, confidence, joy, calm, excitement and belonging, to name a few—and how to intentionally generate these feelings in your life is an important part of creating greater emotional health. Broadening the gaze beyond concerns and survival where possible, assists in restoring a more realistic and balanced perspective generally, reminding us of our resources and the control we actually have.

Prioritising doing things that regularly boost your mood and provide a chance to relax, explore, connect or create, is a powerful way of cultivating increased emotional resilience, healing and health.

TAKEAWAY PRACTICES

- Create a list of activities to include in your life that generate feelings of wellbeing for you. Find ways to put these into practise generally and during times of challenge.

- Look for opportunities in your day to 'bank' positive emotions.

- Practise **Find Three Things** or writing in a **Gratitude Journal** every day for a week and notice the effects of this on your sense of emotional wellbeing.

- Practise **Half Smile Meditation** mindfulness.

'Should you shield the canyons from the windstorms you would never see the true beauty of their carvings.'

Elisabeth Kubler-Ross

Afterword

Emotions are a wonder of being alive, of participating in our life and world. To suffer emotions, to feel overwhelmed or illiterate around our emotional selves, to struggle, is an indictment on the evolution of our humanity. We all deserve to be able to meet the truth of our emotions with skills, insight and accurate knowledge. We all deserve to be able to understand our emotions and have capacity for describing and communicating them to others.

Emotions provide a rainbow of experiences, some desired, some challenging. Nevertheless, all emotion is valuable and deserving of the right context to be held and felt. The value of emotions is frequently lost in society; an ongoing lack of genuine education in understanding, navigating and embracing the gold of emotional truth prevails.

I hope that within this book ideas and information, practices and experiments resonate with the reader, to bridge their own personal divide where needed. Make any helpful information your own; any one thing that you bring into practice that creates change for you, is of value. Leave behind what does not speak to you.

And lastly, I hope that the very nature of our emotions—the capacity to feel—invites acceptance of their *isness* ....

Welcome feeling, welcome your emotional self with awareness, warmth and an appreciation of the importance of emotion to our broader lives.

References

ABC & Vox Pop Labs. (2019). *Australia talks national survey.* ABC. Retrieved from https://www.australiatalks.abc.net.au/

Ainsworth, M., Blehar, M., Waters, E., & Wall, S. (1978). *Patterns of attachment: A psychological study of the Strange Situation* NJ: Erlbaum.

Amthor, F. (2014). *Neurobiology for dummies.* Hoboken, NJ: John Wiley & Sons Inc.

Feldman Barrett, L. (2017). *How emotions are made.* New York: Macmillan.

Holmes, T., & Rahe, R. (1967). The social readjustment scale. *Journal of Psychosomatic Research, 11* (2).

Kless, D., Silverman, P., & Nickman, S. (Eds.). (1996). *Continuing bonds: New understandings of grief.* New York: Francis & Taylor.

Larimer, M., Palmer, R., & Marlatt, G. A. (1999). Relapse prevention: An overview of Marlatt's cognitive behavioral model. *Alcohol Research and Health, 23* (2), pp. 151–160.

LeDoux, J. (1996). *The emotional brain: The mysterious underpinnings of emotional life.* New York: Simon and Schuster.

Linehan, M. (2015). *DBT skills training manual.* (2nd Ed.) New York: Guilford Publications.

Maslow, A. (1943). A theory of human motivation. *Psychological Review, 50* (4) pp.370–396. CiteSeerX 10.1.1.334.7586. doi:10.1037/h0054346

Plutchik, R. (1980). *Theories of emotion.* New York: Academic Press.

Rotter, J. B. (1966). Generalised expectancies for internal versus external control of reinforcement. *Psychological Monographs: General and Applied, 80,* pp. 1–28.

Seligman, M. (2013). *Flourish.* New York: Simon and Schuster.

Surf Life Saving Australia. (2020). *Rip currents.* Retrieved from: https://beachsafe.org.au/surf-safety/ripcurrents

Trampe, D., Quoidbach, J., & Taquet, M. (2015). Emotions in everyday life. *PLoS ONE, 10* (12): e0145450. https://doi.org/10.1371/journal.pone.0145450

Wallin, D. J. (2007). *Attachment in psychotherapy.* New York: The Guilford Press.

Author Bio

Christine Judd grew up in western NSW, Australia, in the mining town of Cobar, aboriginal for 'red or burnt earth'. She has fond memories of a childhood in a small remote outback community, embedded within a vast, dry landscape, where the earth was indeed a rich red ochre.

On leaving school she pursued her strong creative drive by completing a bachelor's degree in visual arts, studying printmaking, painting and drawing.

After a decade living in India in a meditation centre, and travelling widely in Asia and Europe, Christine returned to Australia. She studied counselling and psychotherapy, went on to qualify as a social worker and recently completed her Master of Mental Health Practice. She has worked in not-for-profit community services with people from diverse backgrounds, providing both individual and group therapy. She has experience working clinically in women's health, trauma work, problem gambling and addiction, mental illness, domestic and family violence, and personality disorders. She has worked with people of all ages.

She is now an Accredited Mental Health Social Worker, and currently works in a national counselling service that supports people with mental health concerns as well as those affected by domestic violence and sexual assault. She also works in private practice as a counsellor.

Christine lives in inner-city Sydney with her cat and dog, plays violin, and enjoys long walks in nature. She is passionate about advocating for better emotional health for all, the power of creativity, and the richness of a life truly lived.

Beyond Stormy Weather Free Resources – Values Identification Workbook

———————•••◆◆◆•••———————

Values represent what is important to us in how we live our life and the choices we make. Identifying your values clearly allows you to live in a more fulfilling way and to have a solid sense of self to draw upon.

As a special offer with this book purchase, receive your free Values Identification Workbook.

Utilise the Values Identification Workbook to discover what is important to you.

Access this workbook from: www.christinejudd.com.au/Resources

Christine Judd –
Speaker at your next event

Christine Judd has been working as a therapist for over twenty years. She has a counselling and psychotherapy degree, is an Accredited Mental Health Social Worker and recently completed a Master of Mental Health Practice. She holds certification in Training and Assessment.

Christine has delivered psychoeducation to community groups and professionals while working in the not-for-profit and private sector, covering topics on mental health, gambling addiction, family violence and complex presentations.

She is passionate about equipping people with tailored, accessible information to enhance stress management and emotional wellness. Her approach is friendly and safe, offering practical take-home skills and strategies to her audience.

Topic suggestions:
- ➢ Simple and effective tools for managing emotional stress
- ➢ Tools for emotional fitness (grounding, mindfulness, unhelpful thinking, boosting wellbeing)
- ➢ Understanding emotions
- ➢ Emotional self-care for professionals and staff
- ➢ Any topic covered in the book *Beyond Stormy Weather: Keys for Understanding, Navigating and Embracing Your Emotions*

Talks can be tailored to your needs and timeframe.

Please contact us through www.christinejudd.com.au for further details.

Notes

Christine Judd

Notes

Christine Judd

CPSIA information can be obtained
at www.ICGtesting.com
Printed in the USA
BVHW031353150321
602550BV00001B/195

9 781922 372963